A Nature Diary of th

by

Gordon Waterhouse

To Barbara

with thanks for forty years a-walking together.

ORCHARD PUBLICATIONS

2 Orchard Close, Chudleigh, Devon TQ13 0LR
Telephone: (01626) 852714

ISBN 9781898964810

Printed by
Hedgerow Print, Crediton, Devon EX17 1ES

i

Introduction

For ten years I have written a weekly nature diary for South Hams Newspapers, recording what Barbara and I have seen on our walks. Here is a selection from those 500 articles, following a year from January to December, which I hope will give you pleasure. Copies of all 500, complete with an index, will be available in the Kingsbridge Library for reference purposes.

Thank you to all those readers, past and present, who have stopped to talk with me, telephoned or written in about your sightings and the Nature Diaries. Also to those who have joined us on our rambles and cruises. You have enriched our lives.

Contents

January 1

February 7

March 13

April 19

May 25

June 30

July 37

August 43

September 50

October 56

November 62

December 68

JANUARY

January 6th 1997

The bitingly cold, east winds and low temperatures have brought many birds westwards to Devon over Christmas, hoping like us for a better life in the west. Inland there are flocks of lapwing; black and white plovers with broad wings, a wavering flight and plaintive call of 'pee-wit'. They rest in the higher, flatter fields, their slender crests shaken by the wind. Often they are joined by golden plover, which are smaller, sharp-winged and golden brown.

By the roadsides, where blown leaves hide insects and seeds and seeping moisture softens the iron frosted ground, robins, wrens, blackbirds and thrushes search for food. More common than the song thrushes are the darker redwings; thrushes with a creamy eye-stripe and rusty red flanks, which come each winter from Scandinavia. I have been driving slowly to avoid them as they make suicide dashes in front of the car. The robins especially, barely seem to have the strength to flutter up into the hedge.

Start Valley in snow.

Mick and Linda Hornby saw a woodcock, bracken brown and as big as an owl, by the roadside near Prawle, pushing his long, straight bill into the softer verge.

1

Down on the Kingsbridge Estuary there are over a thousand wigeon duck and several hundred teal – small and fast, the Spitfires of the duck family, also red-breasted mergansers, with their 'punk-style' crests, goldeneye, pochard, shoveler and a few gadwall. There have been two great northern divers, in their traditional feeding area south of the Saltstone and Bill Deakins saw a black-throated diver by New Bridge at Bowcombe.

Last week two avocets, the emblem of the RSPB, arrived and were discovered by Michael Brooking, scything the mud with their up-turned bills in the estuary mud between Embankment Road and Park Bay.

The little egrets are braving out the weather but, instead of high-stepping along the water's edge and darting after shrimps with their needle bills, there were six by the channel below the quay at Kingsbridge, standing motionless and hunched. Will they survive the winter?*

Common gulls are the least common of the four or five species of gull we regularly see on the estuary. More than usual have arrived recently - two or three hundred - but sadly one in three have patches of oil on their bellies. Many will die from ingesting the oil as they try to preen it out of their feathers. The first oil spill disaster was off Devon's coast in 1896. Now, in 1997 the scourge is with us again.

The hazards of winter are with us but the days are lengthening, the snowdrops are in bloom and the fire in the grate flickers a welcome.

* Two weeks later, Dan and Janet Twining found the emaciated body of an egret by Blanksmill Creek.

January 18th 2000

Pollen in January! This week the first hazel catkins are shedding their pollen, wriggling like lambs' tails in the wind. The almond-scented spikes of winter heliotrope have been flowering since before Christmas and now dogs' mercury and snowdrops are joining them.

On Tuesday, Nigel Mortimer took me to see the new pond at Hangar Marsh, by North Sands car park in Salcombe. The JCB driver has already reported mallard on the pond. In eighteen months the reeds and sedges will have clothed the black, peat banks and, from the water, damsel, dragon, caddis and mayflies will be emerging. The swallows will feed on them by day and the bats by night. There is no frogspawn yet, although many ponds already have some. We will all gain pleasure and understanding of nature's tangled web from the Hangar Marsh project – the pond and the wildlife hide.

For our Wildlife Watch Club meeting on Saturday we visited the hide at Beesands. Alice Henderson counted the gulls, over a hundred of them, including black-headed, common, herring, great black-backed and a single kittiwake. There

Snowdrops.

were tufted ducks and pochard diving out on the water but it was Rory Sanders who recognised the shoveler duck, resting by the edge of an island of reeds.

Through the telescopes we watched the drake, saw his white breast and chestnut belly and his contortions as he twisted his long, shovel beak and shining, green head, so he could scratch his 'ear' with a bright orange foot.

Out of the reeds, two coots swam towards each other, like prize-fighters, their smoky-black feathers fluffed up. They pecked at their rival with their white beaks and then lay back and flailed away with their lobed, flip-flop feet for a full minute, as the spray and feathers flew.

On Sunday I was privileged to join Dennis Elphick and Nick Ward, helping to ring the Bowcombe swans. Soft, brown bread was thrown down to them over the wall, while Dennis' team of six slowly encircled the guzzling birds. With military precision but a naturalist's unhurried calm, Dennis organized the advance, until we were within touching distance. Then each of us stretched out one arm to curl around a swan's body, while the other hand gently held its neck. Instantaneously the three brown and white cygnets and their handsome parents were immobilised. Soft bands of cloth were wrapped over the wings, while each was weighed. Rings were put on the legs of the cygnets, so we can follow their future histories. Dick Balkwill, the vet, checked the leg of the penn, who has been limping, and happily found no serious injury; she is doing a good job of raising the cygnets,

3

together with her mate. The recording completed, all five were released at once. They waddled on their huge, webbed feet to the water's edge and set sail, as a flotilla of graceful galleons, out onto the creek.

Ringing the family of swans at Bowcombe with L to R: Barrie Whitehall, Nick Ward, Dennis Elphick and Barbara Henry.

January 25th 2000

The British Trust for Ornithology is surveying winter birds, in random kilometre squares all over Britain. I have been allocated the square between Stokenham and Torcross and I am grateful to the local farmers for giving me access to their land.

One morning this week, I walked round the fields to the south of the A379. Up in the stubble fields, on the high ridge, I disturbed a flock of about 150 linnets. They rose from the stubble and flew, in a tight, bouncing flock, into the tree-tops of a little copse. Linnets, have been decreasing over recent years. From the stubble below the copse, a male cirl bunting, our South Hams speciality, flew up.

The next stubble field was on the wide top of the ridge – very large, very flat and very exposed. I could imagine it as part of the wide steppes of Russia or Kirghizstan. Up flew a rippling flight of skylarks, perhaps thirty. As I walked across the field, more groups of skylarks rose and circled over me, chirruping melodiously - about 90 larks in total. I could see a scattering of cereal grains, green clumps of clover and wind-scorched weeds, such as heartsease, field madder and scarlet pimpernel among the stubble. Nature and the farming regime had created a perfect pick-your-own mixture for these linnets and larks – and for the rare cirl bunting.

My next visit was to the pick-your-own farm, at Stokeley Barton. The hedges there are delightfully varied, a few narrow and manicured, some wide and bushy, some with tall lines of poplar trees and some with no hedge but a line of fence posts where I disturbed a stonechat. Where the field had been ploughed, beside a hedge, several dunnocks, one of the least ostentatious but most promiscuous of British birds, were searching for insect food among the purple clods of soil and with them a tiny, green goldcrest. The best was still to come. When I reached the orchards, feasting on the windfall apples, among the long, green grass were masses of fieldfares and starlings. The starlings took flight, about forty of them flying off in a group, like swift, black fighter planes, but the grey-rumped fieldfares just chuckled an alarm and flew up into the apple trees. Then, in groups of a dozen or more, they rose into the tall poplars; more and more of them until there were over a hundred.

As I scanned the grass under the orchard for more birds, there was a big, sage-green bird with a yellow rump, red crown and red moustaches – a wonderful view of a green woodpecker – and a hundred yards away, from the old trees around Stokeley Manor, a great spotted woodpecker drummed, as if playing on pitched woodblocks – the Ringo Starr of nature's band.

January 17th 2006

Jim Bennett had an amazing experience to start the New Year, on watch duty at Prawle Point lookout. He saw a massed flock of birds about quarter of a mile offshore. He trained the telescope on them and saw it was a mixture of gulls hovering and gannets plunging into a disturbed patch of sea. As he watched, he saw the arching backs of a pod of dolphins leaping around the boiling water. The dolphins had found a shoal of fish, which were also leaping to escape the circling hunters. In his telescope Jim saw a herring gull snatch one small fish in mid-air.

January is the best month to visit our estuaries. We have looked, unsuccessfully, for a laughing gull, an American vagrant that has been seen on the Kingsbridge Estuary recently; one of several seen in Britain this winter. The first Devon record was in 1984 but George Montagu first recorded a laughing gull in Britain in 1774, when he was stationed near Winchelsea.

On 10th January we walked from Frogmore, up the creek to Wareham Point, round Charleton Bay to the hide and Charleton Marsh and finally, after soup at the Ashburton Arms, inland to join the old coach road path back to Frogmore. We saw two greenshanks and lots of redshank, which yelped a warning as a sparrow-hawk flew across the creek. In 'diving duck bay', near Geese Quarry Wood, we found a few goldeneye, great crested grebes and three red-breasted mergansers.

Rough seas near Prawle Point.

Round the foreshore of Charleton Bay there were five rock pipits by the old cart track, where rock pipits have wintered for at least thirty-five years.

On the filter bed of the sewage works, at the top of the marsh, five chiffchaffs were pecking for insects among the chippings. Chiffchaffs are becoming more common as winter visitors. With them was a male blackcap. After lunch we took the footpath up the lovely, wild valley north of Marsh Lane. High overhead, a flock of about 200 golden plover wheeled in the sky. From the overgrown ditch on our right came an unearthly scream – the call of a water rail. By the end of the day we had seen 52 species of bird – a good start to the year.

Sunday was the day of the estuary bird count. The strong wind made viewing through the telescope difficult. Strong winds often bring big numbers of gulls flying down the valley corridor from Torcross to Kingsbridge; we counted 280 great black-backed gulls off the Saltstone. Brent geese are at a record level. Perry Sanders had counted 130 a few days ago, and we had 118. Twenty-five years ago we had the first Brent geese on the estuary. Numbers of pintail ducks are continuing to rise, with at least 35. We didn't see a laughing gull but, when Jo Lapthorne looked through the telescope to count the hundreds of wigeon and teal at the mouth of Blanksmill creek, she gasped in disbelief. "There's an avocet!" she said. And sure enough, swimming and wading among the ducks was a beautiful, elegant white bird, with black accessories and an up-turned bill.

February 15th 1999

Since the end of January, the first green leaves have been sprouting from the hawthorn twigs. Spring and winter are teasing us, hiding behind each other. The tits are still busy at the peanuts and this month a party of long-tailed tits have visited each day; up to seven of them hanging on the peanut feeder at once. Barbara thought their long tails were like lollipop sticks, while Olive and Geoffrey Hodges thought their's were like feathered bumble bees. Ruby Hewitt has goldfinches feeding on her peanuts.

Last Tuesday – during the two day winter of frost, sun and snow – Rod Bone 'phoned. He had something to show me down on the Avon marshes. Ten minutes later I was scanning the marshes with him for a rare bird. Out on the flooded marsh groups of teal were dabbling, squeaking conversationally to each other, flying off over the water between the dark, spiky clumps of rushes and splashing down again in a flurry of silver water.

"I've got it!" said Rod. There, at the far edge of the floodwater was a wading bird. It walked a few paces, stopped and bobbed its head; the typical behaviour of a plover. It had an upright stance, sandy coloured upperparts and white underparts. Across its breast were two black bands, not one like the ringed plover. It was bigger than a ringed plover and with a much longer tail. Rod identified it as a kildeer plover. Kildeers are common in North America and this one must have been blown across the Atlantic by the winter storms.

Later that day, with a spring in my step, Barbara and I went for a splendid walk, in brilliant sun, with Gerry Bentley. We started at Gara Bridge and followed the west side of the river, up to Bickham Bridge. The snowdrops were spread in

Hazel twig with male catkins and female flowers.

drifts along the river bank in Garaland Copse. Where some fallen branches were rotting on the woodland floor, clusters of scarlet elf cups grew. They are bright red cups, an inch or two across. Out of the woods the hazel bushes were hung with catkins. I can never pass them without searching for the female flowers – little, crimson bottle-brushes from which the big hazel nuts will grow.

At Bickham Bridge we crossed to the east side of the river and walked up the lane towards Diptford. Redwings and a few chuckling fieldfares flew up from the grey-twigged ash trees. We walked up the lane to North Huish and from there turned south, past Combe Norris. As we reached the footpath over the fields to Ley Wood, the sun disappeared. Looking behind us, we saw a bank of black cloud coming down from the north, from Dartmoor's rounded hills. In moments the cold wind was hurling a flurry of snowflakes into our faces. We turned our backs to the blizzard and began to walk across the path-field. The snow flew past us; thick white flakes. A buzzard appeared over the hedge and flew over us into the spinning flakes.

We trudged on over the field, mud caking our boots and making them heavy – feeling like arctic explorers.

February 8th 2000

For the dippers at North Mill, on the River Gara, it was already Valentine's day. In pouring rain, I watched the brown water rushing round the projections from the rocky stream-bed. On neighbouring rocky islets stood two dippers, bob-curtseying to each other. In the dim light, I could only just make out the brownish tinge to the head but the white bibs were almost luminously bright. The male flew across to join his mate but every time he approached she flew on to some other boulder. She made several forays into the thick ivy smothering the old mill walls, perhaps prospecting for a nest site.

This site on the Gara, like many sites, is a traditional one. There is a record of a nest site being used for 123 successive years – but not by the same birds! Five years is a good age for a dipper. They are usually faithful to each other, sometimes for life, although they tend to be more solitary during the winter.

Just as the dipper manages to swim and walk under water, the mole can do it though the earth. On Sunday we had a surprise. We arrived at our little church at Buckland Tout Saints to find forty-one mole hills dotted over the green churchyard. In some parts of England there are old churchwardens' accounts, from centuries past, recording 'For the Heades of everie Moulewarpe, one halfpenny.' I do hope our churchwardens don't put a price on his or her head.

With any luck this will be a short burst of digging. During the winter, moles tend to revisit their deeper tunnels, little used since the previous winter. Where there has been subsidence and roof-falls, the mole re-excavates the tunnel and makes vertical shafts up which to push the surplus soil. Using his wide, front paws like a JCB bulldozer blade, he can shift up to six kilogrammes (about 13lbs) in twenty minutes; that is about fifty times his own weight.

He is well-named, for 'moulewarpe' is old English for 'earth thrower'. He can dive into the earth, digging through the turf using a breast stroke technique; once below ground, he continues with something more like the side stroke, pressing forward and down onto the floor of the tunnel with one paw, whilst scooping back earth with the other. The tunnels act as pitfall traps into which worms and insects blunder. The mole patrols the tunnels, at speeds of up to 2 ½ m.p.h., eating a diet mainly of worms. They are regular in their habits. Barbara has noticed one in our garden, digging at the same time several days running. They have three periods of activity in every twenty-four hours and three sleeps.

Had a herd of moles had been in our churchyard? No, just one; a mole's territory extends to a quarter of an acre or more. Moles mostly keep themselves to themselves, except in the mating season. They have an effective contraceptive system. The female only develops a vagina in spring. The males find and mate with a female – a brief encounter – and then, after the young are born in April, the vagina heals up, leaving a faint scar – no more love-making until next March!

The female, who does all the child-rearing, looks after her litter of about four young for a month after they are born. She suckles them from her four pairs of nipples. After this she is as solitary as the male. Moles are aggressive, quarrelsome and solitary – but God made them too.

February 2nd 2004

Lambs are everywhere and our farmers are caring for them, whatever the weather. Three pictures stay in my mind; Neil Fisher carrying a lamb up the track to the new pasture, because it was finding it difficult to keep up with its mother, Clive Morgan surrounded by a sea of ewes, as he spread extra feed in the troughs and Herbie Morgan showing me his nine bouncing orphans, cosy beneath their warming lamp.

The cold snap brought lapwing and golden plover from the snowy north down to one of their traditional sites at Borough Farm. The two days of winter were sandwiched between mild, grey days, with boisterous wind and driving rain. On one of the bright, frosty days we went to Combestone Tor, beyond Venford Reservoir. The reservoir was brimming over, such a contrast to our last visit, in October when it was nearly empty. We walked from the tors at Combestone, past the wind-pruned hawthorn trees and down the path to Combestone Farm. The old buildings and granite walls, beside the green lane, are decorated with lichens and sprouting polypody ferns. We continued down to the meeting of the West and East Dart, the last part being under old oak trees and among mossy boulders, relic of frost-heaved clitter thousands of years ago. We had planned to cross the stepping stones, where the two Darts meet, but the water level was too high. Instead we retraced our steps, uphill to Combestone Tor.

Combestone Tor.

Last week-end was the grand reopening of Runaway Lane, Modbury, by champion walker Amala Williams. Local volunteers and the 'Life into Landscape' project have given the lane a firm surface but taken away none of its atmosphere. Tall beeches, oaks and ashes still overhang the lane; ferns and mosses clothe the steep sides. About two hundred people turned up to see Amala cut the red tape. Most of them joined one of the walks afterwards. One was led by Valerie Belsey, who has made a study of green lanes and recently published a book of 'Green Lane Walks in the South Hams'. For several years Valerie came round South Hams schools, starting with Modbury, getting the children to act out and explore the history and wildlife of a green lane near their school. The children loved it. They rehearsed a play and acted it to the rest of the school and, in the afternoon, walked down the lane. Here we were again but with a class of two hundred!

Despite our mass invasion, the robins kept singing from the bare branches above us. We never travelled for more than a hundred yards without hearing a robin announcing his territory. The green shoots of bluebell leaves were sprouting from the banks. Our boots bruised the new leaves of wild garlic, or ramsons, at our feet and the garlic smell filled the damp air. The fleshy, round leaves of wall pennywort,

10

or navelwort, were spreading on the banks and up the mossy trunks of the trees. This is a real west-country plant. I often call them 'bellybuttons', for their scientific name includes *'umbilicus'* but I had never heard the name that Alice and Jessica Smith taught me – ' pigs' bottoms'; a wonderfully descriptive name and I shall use it for ever. Wall pennywort will never look quite the same for me!

February 28th 2005

The magnolia at Overbecks is a mass of blossom, despite the arrival of winter. Two weeks ago, in mid-February, we saw blackthorn blossom out at Slapton, but this crisp, seasonal weather may have postponed the 'blackthorn winter' until the real one has passed.

In our clean air, black and hawthorn bushes are often smothered in bushy, grey lichens. Two kinds are quite easy to identify: the soft, grey tufts are *Evernia prunastri* (oak moss) – which was ground up with rose petals and used as a powder to whiten wigs, disguise body odour and discourage head-lice! – and the stiff tufts, with flattened stems and round discs at the tips, are *Ramalina fastigiata*. Now is the time to admire the lichens on the thorn bushes, before the new beauty of leaves and blossom covers them.

Lichens are remarkable plants. Beatrix Potter, who wrote *Peter Rabbit* and the other, ever-popular books for children, studied lichens and fungi. In the 1890s, when she was in her twenties she came to the conclusion that a lichen consisted of two organisms – an alga and a fungus – living in a symbiotic relationship. She took her studies to the Royal Botanic Gardens at Kew, where her uncle, Sir Henry Roscoe, was a senior scientist. But she was only a girl and had no academic qualifications; they dismissed her ideas and declined to investigate them. She wrote to the director, saying, "I wish very much that someone would take it up at Kew and try it, if they do not believe my drawings … the things exist and will all be done by the Germans." She was quite right, a few years later a German professor produced a paper and was praised for discovering the true nature of lichens. In 1901 Beatrix Potter published *Peter Rabbit*. For the next twenty years she continued her writing. This year is the centenary of the publication of *Mrs.Tiggywinkle.* She went on to marry, become a sheep-farmer in the Lake District and eventually leave over 4,000 acres of the Lake District to the National Trust – not bad for someone dismissed as 'only a girl'.

Out in the fields, Neil and Mary's lambs are doing well, looking sturdy and playing games of catch-me-if-you-can and four-legged high-jump. A pair of magpies have been acting as nit-nurses for the ewes, sitting on their broad backs and delicately picking out any parasites.

We sat watching the magpies' relatives, the rooks, the other day. We had been swimming at the Kingsbridge Leisure Centre and the upstairs café gives a grandstand view of the rookery. During the winter, most of the forty or so nests from last year have been blown out. There was a lot of activity in the mild, early part of February, when the first pairs began rebuilding. The cold weather may have damped their ardour a little but there were still about a dozen pairs, rearranging twigs and trying the nest cups for size. We counted seventeen nests on 25th February. In the next month, as spring arrives, that number may double or treble.

Blackthorn scrub.

Ramalina fastigiata—lichens on blackthorn twigs.

March 3rd 1998

We were at Salcombe in Overbecks Garden last week, to see the magnificent *Magnolia campbellii* in its full glory. We sat in the 'statue garden' with friends; sat silently just absorbing the beauty of the wide, spreading tree, smothered with great cups of pink and white petals. Many were a foot in diameter. The bronze statue of the young girl, reaching upwards towards its branches, completed the picture. Later we walked beneath the tree, where the trunk – elephant grey, thick, bent and lichened – supports the huge canopy, with difficulty. Above us, the massed, pink blossoms seemed to shine with their own light. Petals drifted down through the branches and settled at our feet; dark pink on the underside and almost white on the upper. Picking one up, I felt the silky smoothness of its texture.

Magnolia at Overbecks and the bronze statue.

This magnificent species of magnolia was first found, in the foothills of the Himalayas, in 1868. Edric Hopkins, who laid out the terraced garden, planted the tree in the year Queen Victoria died, 1901. Since then different owners and gardeners have nurtured it; Mr. and Mrs.Vereker, Otto Overbecks and The National Trust. But it is Tony Murdock, the head gardener, who has brought the whole garden to its present, exciting old age. The garden is always changing and developing, new clearances let in new avenues of light, yet the old and established are cherished. In 2001 we will celebrate *Magnolia campbellii*'s hundredth birthday.

Down on the Kingsbridge Estuary the seal has been seen again, several times. Once it was eating a very large mullet. It seems to follow the fish in with the tide and then slip away to sea, as the tide falls. It reminded me of Atlanta the seal. A seal pup was stranded on the mud flats off Newton Ferrers after strong gales in November 1959. It was rescued and H.G.Hurrell agreed to take on the challenge. His daughter and two sons provided the stomach pump, the liquid food of mixed milk, margarine, fish-meal and cod liver oil (…ugh!) and dedicated nursing that saved its life. For over ten years it enjoyed life as a celebrity in the swimming pool at their home at Moorgate, near Wrangaton.

Later last week we went walking on Dartmoor, up the Erme valley above Piles Copse. As we passed by the wood, we heard the laughing call of a green woodpecker; the yaffle, as it is often called. I remember reading, in a book on Dartmoor published soon after the Second World War, a list of birds that H.G.Hurrell had seen in this old woodland and the green woodpecker was one of the regular species. Fifty year later, the descendants of those woodpeckers are still at Piles Copse.

February saw many surprises. Bob Burridge, the warden of South Milton and South Huish nature reserves, has already seen several wheatears. Wheatears winter in North Africa. In summer, they nest up on Dartmoor, in walls and rocky clitter. I saw the last straggler, on the edge of the moor, in early November. Now, scarcely two months later, they are returning. They and other African migrants have been enticed by spring-like high pressure and southerly winds to migrate early. They may regret it!

March 10th 2003

March 6th was a real spring day. The sun shone and the celandines suddenly began opening their golden stars. A peacock butterfly was basking on an open celandine in Ledstone. Chaffinches were singing. Shelagh Mileson pointed out the first patch of white violets in Ledstone Lane. In the pasture field next to our garden at Sorley Cross twenty magpies were feeding and courting in the sunshine.

By the next day the grey clouds had returned. We walked up the Avon valley from Loddiswell railway station to Bedlime Wood. Monica and Raoul Ameer Ali joined us for part of the walk and showed us the first wood anemones. The

Wild daffodils by the River Avon.

flowers were nodding and scarcely open, the backs of the petal-like sepals gleaming pearl-pink and shaking in the wind. The white drifts of snowdrops were nearly over but along the river bank the wild daffodils were just opening; so much more delicate than most garden varieties. It had rained heavily all morning and the river was opaque with silt. We met Keith Shackleton and he asked if we had seen the goosanders. He sees them regularly, fishing in the river, but they had probably gone elsewhere until the water cleared. From the path, which runs along the old railway track and finishes at Topsham Bridge, you can see the ponds which Keith Shackleton excavated ten years ago. These have matured into rich reservoirs for wildlife. Even in winter the underwater community never stops swimming or crawling around in the violent game of eat or be eaten. Frogs come here in their hundreds to mate and spawn. As we walked by, a heron stretched his long, grey neck and flew up from the side of the pond.

We returned to Silveridge Bridge along the railway track on the west side of the river. By the path were scarlet elf-cups, growing on some moss-covered, rotting branches. February and March are the best times for them; red-lined bowls, an inch or two across, fit for any elf to take a sip of champagne or a morning dip. Another country name for these cup-fungi is 'fairies' baths'.

On Saturday, Sally Henderson organised a great game for the Wildlife

Explorers' Club. We met at Smallacombe, Geoff Baines' lovely, private nature reserve near Moreleigh. In the woodland that Geoff and Peter Morris had planted, Sally had hidden lots of unnatural items including packets of sweets in the shape of juicy bugs. We then went pond-dipping. The children found quantities of frogs' spawn and long strings of toads' spawn, like black pearl necklaces. They caught lots of snails, water boatmen, water hog-lice and caddis-fly larvae, disguised by protective tubes of old weed stems. Someone suggested dipping in the stream as well as in the pond, to compare what we caught. The community was very different – freshwater shrimps, mayfly nymphs and caseless caddis, which set nets to catch prey washed down by the current.

On the way home, towards Woodleigh, we passed a beautiful bank of wild daffodils, just opening among a forest of polypody fern. There is another patch by the lane to Warfleet, near Week, a little way out of Dartmouth. Please do not pick them, for they cheer us all.

March 22nd and 29th 2004

The warm, southerly wind blowing over the Mediterranean, which urged the painted lady butterflies northwards last month, has been working its magic again. Jeff Booth looked out of his sitting room window, at Modbury, and saw a pink bird on his lawn. He noticed its long, down-curved beak. It was a hoopoe. It flew up into an apple tree, with a flash of black and white, chequered wing-pattern, and began preening. Jeff reached for his video camera. The hoopoe flew to another apple tree. Later, Jeff tried to describe the erratic flight – " Its wings were all over the place."

Hoopoe in Jeff Booth's garden.

A buzzard sailed overhead and the hoopoe immediately flopped down into the garden, out of sight, and reappeared when the coast was clear. Hoopoes are rare, spring visitors overshooting their normal breeding areas on the continent. Seldom are more than ten seen each year in Devon.

While Jeff was looking at the hoopoe, Barbara and I were with Bill Tucker at Great Torrington. Bill introduced me to natural history by starting a school bird club, fifty years ago; he was my class teacher and Latin teacher. He would make up humorous stories about imaginary, class exploits, in Latin, and we had to translate them into English, or vice versa. One story I especially remember had me mischievously announcing there was a hoopoe at the bottom of the school garden. In the story, Mr.Tucker stopped the lesson and took the whole class into the garden, only to discover there was no hoopoe; he had been led up the garden path! My first genuine sighting of a hoopoe was on the bird island of Skokholm, when Bill Tucker took a group from the bird club on a week's holiday in 1956. I imagined it all over again, as Jeff Booth described his beautiful garden visitor.......

The royal hoopoe has stayed around Jeff and Diana Booth's garden for two weeks. Barbara and I called and we had a grandstand view. For some time it sat in the hedgerow, silhouetted against the sky and with its crest closed. Then it flew down and, as it landed, raised its crest, like an orange fan opening. It strutted over the lawn, pushing its curved beak into tussocks of grass. Often it would pull out a thick, wriggling earthworm, throw back its head and gulp it down. The black and white zebra stripes on its back and wings made a beautiful contast with the pinkish-grey body. In colour and size it was similar to a jay. A robin and a wren both came to peck for food beside the hoopoe and a rabbit was grazing nearby. The hoopoe took no notice but when a cat appeared, it flew off. If another hoopoe arrived there might be a happy event in Modbury. They have bred in Britain about forty times in the last hundred years.

Hoopoes have a novel way of protecting their young from predators, both the female and the young have scent glands, which produce a disgusting smell. When this is added to the smell of the droppings, which are not removed from the nest, the hoopoe's nest becomes very uninviting. The hoopoe was the king of the birds in Aristophanes' play, *The Birds*, which he wrote in 414BC. His two main characters, Hopeful and Trusting, wanted to escape the pressures of modern life in Athens and asked the hoopoe to set up a kingdom 'Cloud-cuckoo-land', between earth and heaven, where they could live with the birds. As I watched the hoopoe, I was in 'Cloud-cuckoo-land' – or was it Heaven?

March 28th 2006

Henry Williamson loved wild, spring days in the South Hams. He came regularly to stay at Torcross and loved nothing better than to walk up 'The Line' buffetted by the wind, rain rattling against his coat and the sound of waves roaring on the shingle. He describes this in a book he wrote about travelling his adopted county – *On Foot in Devon*. Meryl Docker told me a sad story about an otter last week. Henry Williamson's most successful work was '*Tarka the Otter* – his joyful water-life and death', written eighty years ago; the tale Meryl told me had all the pathos of a Henry Williamson story.

An otter was found run over on the road near Ugborough Garage. The body was taken to the research station at Starcross, where they carried out an autopsy.

The otter was a young female. She had given birth, probably less than twenty-four hours before, and her breasts were full of milk. Somewhere, perhaps in a holt by the Lud Brook, two or three blind cubs were mewing and slowly starving to death.

The otter hounds that Williamson described are no more and our rivers are cleaner but the world still has dangers for an otter; roads are busier and a new, sometimes fatal variety of liver fluke has been found in some otters. Take care when driving on our roads at night, in case an otter tries to cross your path, and if you find a dead otter contact Ellie Bremner of Devon Wildlife Trust's county records department, on 01392 279 244 and she will arrange for it to be taken to Starcross.

Wheatears – little birds, standing upright like sandy and grey coloured robins, with a white rump - have been arriving from North Africa; some will be on their way to Greenland or Iceland, some will nest among the clitters of Dartmoor. Brenda Child was looking at a party of four on the windswept promontary of Berry Head, when she realised that one had rings on its legs; blue above white on one leg and blue above an aluminium ring on the other. I telephoned the ringing office at the British Trust for Ornithology and they checked their records. The bird was ringed on the Clee Hills in Shropshire in the summer of 2004, since then it has spent two winter-sun holidays by the Sahara Desert. Any day now it will arrive back in the Clee Hills and someone will say, "The white arses are back!"

Other migrants are moving in. On March 25th, three days earlier than last year, Rod Bone saw his first swallow over the River Avon. Dennis Dawes watched a short-eared owl quartering the Avon marshes in mid-March. They are wonderful, day-flying owls with a buoyant flight.

At home our resident tawny owls have been calling every night recently. Barn owl numbers have been recovering. Richard Harding has seen one hunting by Stokenham Church, Margaret Henderson saw one at Chillington and Rod Bone at Aveton Gifford. Their slow recovery has been helped by the work of David and Fran Ramsden and their team at the Barn Owl Trust, providing nest boxes and giving advice – 'Restoring the balance.'

APRIL

April 15th 1997

Skylarks are birds we all remember from our childhood, soaring into a spring-blue sky and raining down heavenly music. Although skylarks have decreased by about 50% in lowland Britain during the last twenty years, the South Hams still has many pairs. I am joining in a nation-wide survey of skylarks. I spent a beautiful morning, last week, exploring one of the kilometre squares that I had been assigned. It was typical of many parts of the South Hams. The higher fields were flatter with corn or silage crops, below them the land fell away into steep combes, with good grazing for sheep, patches of gorse and some oak woodland. At the bottom flowed streams edged by alder and pussy willow.

The farmer had already done several hours work, when I saw him at eight o'clock. He gave me permission to explore off the footpaths and told me where I could find the skylarks.

Above a field of spring corn, a lark was already singing; higher, higher, a mere dot with quivering wings. A pheasant crowed and ruffled his feathers noisily. Along the Devon hedge, every twenty yards or so a robin was singing. From a taller bush a great tit sang, 'Teacher, teacher, teacher.'

Walking down into a combe, I stopped by a clump of gorse. Its rich, gold blossom gave off a sweet smell of rare spice and coconut oil. A few yards from me, in the gorse bush, were two cock yellowhammers. One flew at the other with fluttering wings and there was a flurry of bright yellow breasts and golden heads. Their crown feathers were raised, threateningly. Their rust-brown rumps and white tail feathers showed as one chased the other away. Mr Irish of Edmeston used to call them 'golden laddies' – a fine Devon name.

From the stream a pair of mallard rose, quacking as they flew. The sun caught the drake's green head. I stopped to listen to the soothing sound of the stream flowing over shillet. From the pussy willow and bramble scrub came the 'chiff-chaff, chiff-chaff' of a chiffchaff and a burst of blackcap song, both birds probably newly returned from a winter by the Mediterranean.

Suddenly above me, over the old quarry, came the exciting sound of peregrine falcons. I saw two, sharp-winged birds chasing each other, twisting and climbing. First high, against the blinding sun, and then lower, through the leafy tops of some poplar trees. In flight, they turned, linked talons and fell away, making a yickering scream before regaining composure and speeding away out of sight; the mastery of the bird!

We have been away for a few days and returned to Devon to see the swallows are back to their summer homes. I met Roger Pickles of Modbury, who said, full of excitement, "Our swallows are back and I know they are the same ones as last year!" I am sure he is right.

April 17th 2001

Ryan put out the birds' nests in Buckland Tout Saints church, six, sugar-coated, chocolate eggs into each cake-cup. They looked just like real birds' eggs. He placed the paper nests by the primroses in front of the choir stalls.

The next morning was Easter Day and we had a service of celebration. Things did not go according to plan. As we filed up to take holy communion, I looked down at the eggs. They were shiny and wet; the sugar coating had liquified in the cool, damp atmosphere. After we had taken communion, Peter, our Easter Day priest, whispered in my ear, "Ants!"

Whilst we were sipping the communion wine, in remembrance of the first Easter, the red ants were having their own Easter communion, sipping the sticky sugar from the eggs. The idea was that the children should distribute an egg to each of the adults, after the service, and then eat the rest themselves. We carefully brushed off the ants and the children offered the eggs around. Not surprisingly, the adults didn't seem very keen but the children ate them almost as eagerly as the ants had done.

This was the second near disaster of the morning. Earlier, the children had gathered around the Easter garden, which was on one of the window ledges. Figures of Christ's friends were placed around the open tomb and Mary Magdalene was kneeling before the figure of Christ; the scene on Easter morning, set amongst stones, mosses and ferns. When we arrived at church, I had noticed that a tortoiseshell butterfly had woken from hibernation and was fluttering in the window, behind the Easter garden; "How appropriate," I thought.

But, as we gathered by the window, the butterfly's fluttering became frantic. We saw that its legs had become entangled in some strands of spider-web and it was struggling, desperately to escape. From the mossy hills in the Easter garden, a plump, brown spider rushed forwards on its eight, nimble legs. In a moment it would sink its fangs into the butterfly's body. I pounced and swept up butterfly, spider, web and all. Amy took the butterfly into her caring hands, folding them gently around the trembling tortoiseshell. We all went out into the churchyard and I released the spider into the long grass, to search for a different breakfast. Amy opened her fingers and the butterfly, surprised but unhurt, spread its wings, waited a second and flew from the open tomb into the sunshine. It rested for a while on the grass, so we could all admire it, and then flew off over the churchyard wall on the first day of its resurrected life. It was a close shave!

Now that certain sections of the coastal path are open, Barbara and I walked from Torcross to Beesands. The first sea campion and thrift flowers are out, along with the primroses, celandines and rampant Alexanders. Sand martins and swallows were swooping over Slapton and Widdicombe leys. Great crested grebes were displaying, swimming up to each other face to face, like a couple of elegant book-ends. Sandwich terns – also known as sea-swallows – and kittiwakes were dancing over the blue sea.

Waves on Torcross Beach, where sea-swallows and kittiwakes dance.

April 15th 2002

Our friendly postmen are wonderful. Their early start means they see more wildlife than most of us. One leaned out of his van and called to me, "I see you missed the hoopoe near Ilton Castle."

This week we have visited two farms and a hotel which sum up so much of what is good about the South Hams and why people don't just pay one, fleeting visit, like the hoopoe, but keep coming. Muriel and Ronald Hallett showed us round their farm at Pollardscombe. The cattle and sheep were thriving thanks to Dr Green – the fresh, green grass of springtime. Over the grass leys, skylarks were singing; we watched one mounting higher and higher until it was a fluttering dot against a wisp of white cloud and we could barely hear the reeling song. Ronald once came across a brood of young larks, at the edge of a field, frozen still for safety. Over the valley three buzzards wheeled. A few years ago, Ronald counted more than forty circling. Grazing in another field were about twenty sheep. With a quiet word, Ronald sent the sheep dogs racing off to round them up, so we could have a closer view. The black-faced flock of young Suffolk rams came trotting towards us, although, as Ronald explained, they were still "a bit

21

hippity-hoy, neither man nor boy!"

Mr and Mrs Hallett have helped educate many families who have come on farm holidays. One family came for seventeen years; the children would always clean off their boots before helping Mr Hallett with the milking but on the last day they would leave their boots unwashed, so that they could take a bit of Devon back home with them.

On Saturday the Watch Club went to Jill and Harry Kerswell's farm at Bearscombe. We had a wonderful morning. We were invited to see the quads, which several of us thought were four-wheeled motor-bikes, but turned out to be four healthy lambs only two weeks old, taking it in turns to suckle from their patient mother. Her silky, cream fleece hung down in ringlets and the white lambs gambolled around her. We followed the bridle path up the valley and felt quite puffed out after climbing the hill. We stopped to catch our breath. Harry Kerswell has no trouble with hills, he ran the London Marathon a few years ago, raising over £1,000 for charity. At the end of the morning he helped a ewe give birth, as we watched. Devon farmers are masters of many trades.

Spring squills growing on grassy hummocks near Bolt Tail.

Barbara and I are planning to climb Ben Nevis and one of our training walks was a brisk circuit, up the footpath from St.Clement's Church, Hope Cove, down past the rookery and streamside hamlet of Bolberry and along the coast path to

Bolt Tail. On the grassy hillocks near Bolt Tail, we saw the curly, green leaves of spring squill and its pale blue, star-like flowers. Back at Hope Cove we climbed the steps up to the Cottage Hotel and enjoyed a good, lunchtime snack and a lovely view. A rock pipit pecked for crumbs at our feet.

As we drove home, past Elston Cross, we looked out for the hare that Trudy Thorning saw last week. Well spotted, Trudy.

Hope Cove.

April 5th 2004

The hoopoes have gone. There was another, only seven miles from the one in Modbury. It had spent a week along Hilary and Tony Soper's drive.

Modbury still has a rosy starling. Gloria Hannaford has seen this beautiful bird in her Modbury garden and reports that it has been around for some time. It is similar to a starling, perhaps a little stouter, mostly black but, like a cloak around its neck, the shoulders and belly are dusky pink. There have been more rosy starlings in Britain recently; about fifty each year for the last four years. Some, like Gloria's bird, have stayed. Traditionally their home is in the steppes east of the Black and Caspian Seas. When locusts swarm, the rosy starlings follow them and sometimes travel far from their homeland.

I have yet to hear a cuckoo, or see a swallow but the chiffchaffs are singing their two note celebration of spring, often perched in a pussy willow. The silver or yellow catkins of the pussy willow, which resemble little rabbit scuts, attract the spring bumble bees by day and the moths at night. The weather greatly affects the numbers and varieties of moths that fly each night. I had the moth trap running on a clear, windy night recently. The next morning there were no March moths or dotted borders, light-bodied species, but only a few dumpy, thick-bodied Hebrew characters and common quakers; tough characters and lovely, religious-sounding names.

Karen Ballantine has had an otter which somehow found its way into their garage at Loddiswell. It is such good news that otters are making a come-back and many of the sightings seem to confirm that they travel a lot between one stream system and another; they have been found as road casualties near Stokenham, Salcombe and Thurlestone. Karen 'phoned the RSPCA and her sons Tom and Peter helped the RSPCA lady put the confused otter into a carrying cage. They took it down to the Avon, by New Bridge, and watched it come cautiously out of the cage, slip down the bank into the water and swim away.

Otters regularly visit the head of Bowcombe Creek. On Sunday afternoon I met Michael and Angela Lidstone being taken for an excursion down the creek by their daughter Hannah. By the edge of the tide was a pair of shelduck, dozing, with red bills tucked under the white duvets on their shoulders. A single red-breasted merganser, diving in midstream, was the only winter visitor left. Leaning over the wall we could see the swans had begun moulding the cup of their new nest. On the wall itself was a miniature world of lichens; apple-green, pearly-grey and brown and some a forest of tiny wine-glasses.

At home it was time to hoe the deep brown furrows to plant the potatoes. On the bare earth two speedwells are spreading. The ivy-leaved speedwell is a native and has pale blue flowers and ivy-shaped leaves. It dies away in the summer. The Persian, or field speedwell has bright blue flowers. It was first recorded in Britain in 1825 and comes from Persian lands afar – the lands of the rosy starling. Now it is the most common speedwell in our fields and vegetable gardens.

As I leaned on my hoe, a snowstorm of blackthorn petals was swept from the hedge and the last snowflakes of 'blackthorn winter' danced around me.

Blackthorn in winter.

24

May 5th 1998

In May, on the first Sunday, Buckland Tout Saints Church holds a Rogation service. We walk round the parish asking for a blessing on the land and on all those that work on it. This year we started by the stream at Goveton. From under the stones a small fish darted, while we were singing about streams of living water. It was probably a stone loach, a mottled, grey-brown fish that has cat-like whiskers around its mouth. Pauline Mitchell used to catch them in her cupped hands, in this same stream fifty years ago. Her name for them was 'catabirds'.

The next part of our service was near a farmyard. Between every phrase of the prayer or hymn, the bleating lambs and their deep-voiced mothers would add their own 'amens' from the pasture field. A chaffinch offered his short song, over and over, from a hawthorn bush dappled with cream may blossom. From across the village a song thrush shrilled his echoing notes as a descant.

Buckland Tout Saints Church.

The birds continued singing as we walked down to a cottage garden, admiring its flowers and thinking of all those gardeners who are busy sowing and planting. For the next stop, we had to climb the hill, up the winding lane. The flowers along the hedge-banks were as beautiful as those in the gardens. We admired the shining, scalloped leaves and bright pink flowers of the shining cranesbill. Among the grasses, the stitchwort and the red campion, were also the spiked cowls of lords and ladies. The roots of lords and ladies were used to make starch in Elizabethan times; it served to stiffen the ruffs and lace around the necks of the gentry. It has a wealth of descriptive names, several of which are vulgar. The purple, or occasionally yellow, spadix, which sticks up in the sheathing spathe, looks rather phallic and this is the origin of the old name – 'cuckoo pint'; pintle being a slang term for penis. 'Willy lily' is a modern name with the same origin. Botanically it is *Arum maculatum*; 'maculatum' means spotted and the arrow-shaped leaves often have black spots. My favourite name is 'Kitty-come-down-the-lane-jump-up-and-kiss-me'.

By the time we had climbed to the field gate, through which we could see a fine barley crop sprouting, we were out of breath. The skylark, singing far above us over the barley field, seemed never to stop for breath. In the hedge, down at our feet, the sticky goosegrass was beginning to clamber upwards, through and over the other plants. The stickiness is caused by thousands of little hooks, like Velcro, that enable the weak and floppy goosegrass to climb so efficently. Crawling on the goosegrass, oblivious of our prayers for creatures great and small, was a round, black beetle as big as my finger-nail – a bloody-nose beetle. He too has his place in creation, feeding on the leaves of goosegrass and its relations.

So finally we reached the church on the hilltop, sang our last hymn and looked out at the South Hams in Maytime. If only May could last twice as long.

May 18th 1998

We had a field day for those on our Wildlife of the Coast course. Early morning mist began to lift, as we arrived at Prawle. We walked down to Horseley Cove, admiring the view of the rocky shore and the rippled sea. In the steep, sunken path we saw butterflies; holly blues fluttering like wind-blown blossom and a pair of brown and gold speckled woods, flying a courtship slalom around us.

From the hedge in front of us came a short rattle of birdsong. We stopped and listened. The song was a cirl bunting's. Soon all the group could see the bird; black and yellow striped head, black bib, green breast. I was still looking. "Not there, Gordon, it's only about eight feet away!" I put aside my telescope.

Down on the beach we spent an hour looking in the rock pools and under the seaweeds. Pat Davidson found a Cornish sucker-fish, which has oval, false eyes, rather like a peacock butterfly's. We also found a worm pipe-fish, with the snout of a seahorse, to which it is related. We left the weeds, the winkles and the crabs and made our way back to the cliff path. Out at sea a gannet flew lazily past, stalled in mid-air and plunged into the waves.

The pink globes of thrift were speckling the cliff-top and the kidney vetch, or 'ladies' fingers', spread clouds of yellow.

Across the path we saw several oil beetles, very long, black beetles with small wing-cases not covering the segmented abdomen. These fascinating creatures have larvae that crawl on to certain solitary bees, hitch a lift back to their nest and finish their development by feeding on the bee's eggs and store of nectar and pollen.

We finished our morning walk by climbing up to Prawle Point and continuing round to Elender Cove. As it is sheltered by the rocky promontory of Gammon Head, the cliffs round the cove provide good nest sites for birds. We saw many herring gull nests and four shags sitting on their cliff-ledge nests – dizzy perches.

We had our picnic lunch overlooking the cove. Philip le Houx suddenly cried out for he had seen three dolphins leap from the water and plunge back. We all watched as two more surfaced and then saw the original three arch out of the water again, their dorsal fins curved scimitars.

The afternoon might have been an anti-climax but it certainly was not. We walked round Mattiscombe, by Peartree Point towards Start Point. We saw a seal at Peartree Point. Shortly afterwards we heard the 'seven whistler' call of some whimbrel and there, walking daintily through a cliff-top patch of massed bluebells, were a flock of six whimbrel. The curved bills and dark-striped heads stood out above the bluebells, silhouetted against a turquoise sea.

We eventually arrived at South Hallsands. Delicious tea and cakes at Trouts, to the accompaniment of the Hallsands kittiwake choir, completed a perfect day.

May 9th 2000

With Byan and Jane we were off to see the 'pelicans' at Burgh Island. We walked across the isthmus of sand that links the island to Bigbury-on-Sea. Once up the slipway and past the Pilchard Inn, we took the path along the western side, climbing steadily. The grassy slopes down to the rocky shore on the right were white-washed with white clouds of sea campion. Suddenly the path stopped climbing and ended at a precipice. The gusty wind pushed, treacherously, at our backs. Far below were grey sea and jagged rocks set like an uneven row of broken teeth. Rising almost level with us was a giant tower of rock - a sea stack. There were occasional ledges on the vertical walls and here curly-crested shags had built their nests of seaweed and driftwood twigs. In spite of the sunless weather, the sitting birds gleamed with a green iridescence. One stood up and revealed two or three small, black powder-puffs – young chicks.

Meanwhile our wives stood waving and calling but the wind blew away their words. Only when we had joined them and looked down did we really share their excitement, for they had found the 'pelicans'.

Two ridges of white-washed rock sloped out from the cliff down towards the sea. Their rugged profiles were dramatic. Along the crests, on exposed ledges,

From Burgh Island, sea campion and thrift with Bantham beyond.

were about twenty nests, bigger and more untidy than the shags'. At each were several long-necked birds – two or three brown ones, which were well-grown young, and one or two blue-black parents.

The adults had bronze mantle and wings; each bronze feather was edged with black, giving the appearance of metallic scales – half bird, half dragon. Both young and adults had green eyes, stout, hooked beaks and loose skin hanging beneath their chins. The young would vibrate this flabby skin, as they made high-pitched, begging calls for food. The adult's pouch, just like a real pelican's, provided a storage bag for the fish soup, which was food for the young.

Occasionally, one of the young would thrust its entire head into its parent's gullet for a serving of soup. Raising their tails was a signal for a fountain of liquid droppings to shoot out of the bird's back-passage and spray the rock-face and any birds below.

Were these creatures pelicans or pterodactyls? Neither, they were cormorants of course. The name is derived from the French 'corneille marin' - crow of the sea - but they are not related to crows; cormorants, shags, gannets and frigate birds all belong to the pelican family.

A few days later, when summer had arrived, Donald Dykes took us to the grassy promontory at the very end of the island. Tufts of pink thrift were mixed with the sea campion. A great black-backed gull was on its nest there and many herring gulls. There was a panoramic view of the cormorant colony and, on the towering stack beyond, a peregrine sat – lord of his domain.

May 3rd 2004

In Andrew's Wood, Bluebell Clearing is at its best. Spring is bursting and the birdsong getting louder and more varied. Will a tree pipit arrive this month? There used always to be a few pairs nesting in the grassy clearings. I will always remember the occasion when Chris Pierce and Bryan Ashby were photographing from a hide and saw an adder attack a nestful of nestlings. The hungry reptile returned through Chris' hide. For other reasons, tree pipits have been declining and we did not hear any in Andrew's Wood last year.

Sharing one's enjoyment of a special place always adds to the experience. Chris Pierce, Barrie Whitehall and Fiona Woolmer joined me on three visits. Highlights were the twittering of linnets sat on gorse bushes in Top Clearing, a pair of marsh tits passing within a yard of us, chiffchaffs and willow warblers carrying grass and feathers to build their nests, a great spotted woodpecker pecking out his nest-hole and a pair of tree creepers flying a slalom around the trees, playing catch-me-if-you-can.

One afternoon Barbara took me to Thurlestone and we walked along the coast path to Hope Cove. The yellow flowers of kidney vetch – ladies' fingers – were already out and the pink globes of thrift on their slender stems, waving in the breeze. A long, black oil beetle crawled across the path in front of us and several globular, black, bloody-nose beetles.

We walked across Thurlestone Sands, where the sand had built up and blocked off the stream where it flows out of South Milton Ley; the canyon of a few months ago was completely filled.

On South Huish Marsh were a few mallard, a pair of shelduck, some coots and moorhens and just six teal, passing through on migration. Several swallows swooped over the shallow water and perched in pairs on the telegraph wires. There were clumps of bluebells by the path, many of them with Spanish bluebell genes, with bigger and more upright bells than our native bluebells.

Clumps and avenues of the green-yellow Alexanders – said to have been introduced by the Romans – are at their best now. The heavy scent attracts squadrons of black, assassin flies, also known as St.Mark's flies, for St.Mark's day is April 25th, when the flies often emerge.

We varied our return route. Instead of walking across Thurlestone Sands we walked across the National Trust car park. The early scurvy-grass flowers, which have been scattered like salt by the coastal paths and inland motorways, are nearly over but, by the ramp that leads down to the beach, another member of the cress family is growing – hoary cress. This is taller and has creamy-white flowers. It is reputed to have been introduced by our soldiers emptying their straw mattresses on Kentish shores, after their campaign in the Dutch Friesian islands during the Napoleonic wars.

June 9th 1998.

This is a really good foxglove year. Many of the purple spires are nearly as tall as a man, each with about a hundred purple thimble flowers. Along the hedge banks and especially where the ground was disturbed a year or two ago, they are magnificent. Foxgloves are biennials, growing a rosette of leaves in their first year and sending up the flower stem in the second. The flowers open in sequence, starting at the bottom. This extends their flowering season and helps with the process of pollination. Look at one of the freshly fallen, tubular flowers and you will see the neat arrangement of four stamens on the roof and a floor patterned with dark spots and white rings, which merge to form a white pathway to the nectar source. From the floor, long, white hairs bend inwards to let insects find their way in but hinder their exit. As they wriggle their abdomens, pollen from the stamens is brushed onto their backs. The stamens ripen first, so the upper, newer flowers have the pollen. In the lower flowers, the slender, fork-tipped stigma matures and droops down from the roof. In this position, the backs of the bumble and honey bees brush against it. Look at the bees and you will see that they usually start by visiting the lowest flowers, so cross pollination is achieved.

There has been drama down on the Kingsbridge Estuary this week. At Bowcombe, two weeks ago, the swans hatched nine eggs. The same day as the pair on Collapit Creek hatched seven. On Saturday, the Bowcombe pair swam, with their nine fluffy, grey cygnets in line, a mile across the estuary to Collapit. There the Bowcombe cob attacked the Collapit cob, leaving him covered in mud and bleeding from the head. During the commotion, the cygnets of both pairs mingled and, whether by design or accident, the Bowcombe pen had added four to her brood by the time the Collapit cob had escaped back to his family. He limped, with his pen and their remaining three cygnets, up from the creek into the lane and started to lead them up the tarmac towards Kingsbridge. Jeannette and Tony Tabb have always kept a friendly eye on the Collapit swans.

Peter and Margaret Quick and I came to join the onlookers. We saw where the cobs had fought; huge, webbed footprints in the churned-up mud. The Collapit cob was standing by his pen, preening, recovering his composure and taking wet, wholemeal bread-crumbs from Tony, while three remaining cygnets dabbled in the stream, pecking at weed. A hundred yards downstream we saw the Bowcombe pen standing in the main channel, with thirteen cygnets. All appeared unconcerned by the change in their family arrangements. The cob stood on guard a few yards away.

The next morning the Collapit birds moved to Blanksmill Creek and the Bowcombe pair took the thirteen cygnets back to Bowcombe.

Roger Swinfen, who has been ringing swans in Devon for thirty years, had never heard of this but, at Abbotsbury the swanherd told me that pairs often gather extra cygnets; one brood grew from six to twenty-five!

June 29th 1999

Under the shelter of the wall at Bowcombe Creek, the pen swan was sat on her nest. Nestling against her side, basking in the sun, were two cygnets. One stretched out a grey foot and spread the webs; its sibling pecked at the foot in curiosity. It was a scene of domestic bliss, with the cob standing on the shore beside the nest. Then the cob extended his long neck and hissed – a crow hopped out from behind the nest and flew away. Another crow flew down towards the nest and both parents lifted their heads and hissed threateningly.

Domestic bliss was an illusion. One of those crows had already taken a cygnet and they were waiting for the chance to take another. The swans' marriage was a recent and unconventional one. Having lost his wife in the autumn, he has paired with one of his own daughters from several seasons ago. We could tell this from the rings on their legs.

With permission from Slapton Ley Field Centre, Bryan Ashby and Chris Pierce have watched a pair of reed warblers from the time the eggs were laid in a deep hammock of a nest, suspended among the swaying reeds. On 17th June the first egg hatched and by the next day all four had emerged – minute, purple-pink scraps of skin, with a yellow beak at one end. Every few minutes throughout the day, the parents have been feeding them. At night and when the weather is cold the mother will sit on the nest, brooding her young. Bryan and Chris have taken many photos. When I last saw them they were eight days old and ready to leave the nest within a few days. By September they will be flying to Africa for the winter, joining their parents. In the 19th century reed warblers spread around Britain as

A dormouse in Andrew's Wood.

a breeding species and they first arrived at Slapton Ley in the 1860s.

Last week I also had the privilege of joining Tom Maddock, checking the fifty boxes put up in Andrew's Wood as part of a national survey of dormice. Whereas most of the birds are on their way to raising their first or even second family of the year, the dormice have hardly begun to think about it. Most of the eight dormice we found were fast asleep, completely torpid, their rusty-gold bodies curled up and their tails wrapped over their pink noses. Twice we found husband and wife in bed together but we scarcely disturbed their dreams. It will probably be August before we see litters of babies. The pigmy shrews we saw in one box were very different; they already had a litter of tiny babies, as pink-purple and naked as the reed warblers' nestlings.

Some of these bright, June mornings have been too beautiful to stay asleep. The grass-heads have grown tall and are nodding with the weight of dew. New flowers are out on the hedgebanks; the delicate, white stars of lesser stitchwort and the tall, pale-pink common valerian, which prefers the wetter, often north-facing banks.

June 6th 2000

The story of the tree creepers that nested in Dan Twining's experimental tree creeper box (Box E.T.C.) began on the 13th April – unlucky for some but a red letter day for us.

Tree creeper.

Hide.

Chimney Sweeps.

At first the nest was just a few chips of rotten wood and some thin twigs. A week later there was a proper little besom broom of twigs – bramble, birch and bracken. By the 30th, there was a grass and feather lining – the female's task – with two, white, red-speckled eggs. All six eggs had been laid by 7th May.

Bryan Ashby, Chris Pierce and I made plans to put up a hide, ready to take photographs. On the evening of the 10th May we put up the first part of the steel tower on the left side. Each day we built a little more, so the mother bird, who does all the incubation, would grow accustomed to the weird tent on stilts.

We expected the eggs to hatch on about the 19th May, fifteen days after the last egg was laid. On the 15th Chris sat in the hide and I watched, from about twenty yards away. Within a minute the brown, mouse-like bird landed on the trunk, below the nest box and crept up the right hand side in short jerks.

On Sunday morning, 21st May, I went up to the nest box and opened it carefully. Inside were a cluster of nestlings – not naked, pink-purple babies but downy black ones, like a brood of chimney-sweepers. That afternoon Chris watched both parents shuffling up the trunk, their slender, black beaks crammed with insects and spiders to feed their young and over the next few days Bryan, Chris and I spent many hours cramped into that hide.

Sometimes both birds would arrive together and pause. Then Bryan or Chris would get a lovely shot of the silvery breast, the streaky brown and buff upperparts and the white eye-stripe, with a kink in it which gives them such a quizzical expression. They scuttled up the trunk, leaning backwards on stiff, pointed tail feathers. We grew to love those devoted parents.

By the 28th May the young were feathered – pale versions of their parents but with shorter, yellow beaks and a Mohican crown of black down By the 2nd June they looked almost ready to fly. The normal fledging period is fifteen days. When I peeped in on the 4th June – the fifteenth day – I thought I had found a nestful of miniature bitterns; all six fledglings raised their heads, necks and long, curved beaks skywards and froze. I quietly closed the box and walked away through the sunlit wood, pleased to have shared a success story with those model parents from Box T.L.C.

June 4th 2001

The mistle thrush in Wolfgang and Frances Link's garden started a special year for us; '2001 – A Garden Odyssey'. Wolfgang found a mistle thrush nesting in a cypress tree by his garden shed. We were invited to photograph the mistle thrushes. They were star performers, bringing great mouthfuls of worms and stuffing them down the gaping throats of the very plump nestlings. Wolfgang and Frances' garden is a paradise for birds and whoever was not in the hide watching the thrushes was walking round the garden looking for other nests.

In mid-April we saw a chiffchaff carrying a strand of dead grass. Following its route, through shrubs and ferns, Chris found a beautifully domed nest. A few days later it had laid its eggs and begun sitting. Most small birds incubate their eggs for two weeks and feed their young another two weeks before fledging.

The chiffchaffs were soon feeding their young, with black bundles of squashed

Cock greenfinch with young.

Spotted flycatcher leaving after feeding his mate.

Cock bullfinch and some of the 'choir'.

Mistle thrush and a diet of worms.

insects every two or three minutes. They would hover in front of the domed nest, like olive-green humming birds, then down on the ground and push their heads inside the nest.

Bryan, Chris and Wolfgang found nests of robin, dunnock, greenfinch and goldfinch. Hides were appearing everywhere. While tending a flower bed beneath the huge Monterey pine, Wolfgang saw a goldfinch and hidden among the tufts of long, dark pine needles was a neat nest of woven roots, hair and feathers. Chris and Bryan slowly built up a hide on stilts, so they could watch from only six feet away. Two young hatched and we watched the parents, pushing through the dark foliage, their ivory bills surrounded by crimson and white faces, regurgitating half-digested seeds into the red gapes of the chicks. Unlike most small birds, that neatly dispose of the fledglings' droppings, the goldfinches' excreta built up like dribbling icing around the edge of a birthday cake.

The greenfinches had better sanitory arrangements. Their nest was in a spiky cypress. Bryan had been the first to take photographs, when the young were blind and naked. He caught the male, brilliant with yellow wing flashes and green head and breast, feeding the four scraps of day-old nestlings; their skinny, red necks rose together, supporting each other and four bright orange mouths opened together, like some exotic flower. Two weeks later the young had grown into teenage thugs – jostling each other and aggressively demanding food from their distraught looking mother. She must have been glad when they left home!

In an unused garage we found a pair of spotted flycatchers had built their nest on a ledge, next to an old packet of Polyfilla – a sponsored bird's nest! Another hide was constructed and we watched the male bringing food to his mate, who incubated the eggs, and then both birds feeding the newly hatched young. Before coming to the nest itself, they would land on a hanging loop of wire and it would swing gently to and fro, with the spotted flycatcher enjoying the ride. Sadly, a visiting cat climbed up and took the young from the nest.

The story of the bullfinch's nest had a happy ending. Bullfinches mate for life and continue to live together even through the winter. When their five young hatched, they came as a pair to feed the fluffy, brown, rather frog-like fledglings, she in subtle shades of brown and grey and he with bright pink waistcoast. All five young fledged successfully. At the end of our garden odyssey, the three boys who went birdsnesting had broad, satisfied grins on their faces. Thank you Frances and Wolfgang!

July 28th 1997

The swallows in our garage have another family. This time they have only a 'pigeon pair'; Bryan and I have been photographing them from his hide. Both mother and father feed the young. They sweep into the darkness and turn upwards to grasp the rim of the mud-made nest. For a moment she holds her wings out and backwards; a beautiful archangel arriving with the heavenly food of squashed insects. The chick that begs most vociferously is fed. The parent bends forward towards the open mouths and thrusts its own head right inside to regurgitate the food down the scrawny throat of the nestling.

Swallow, an archangel with heavenly food.

At first the parents removed the faecal sacs but, as the chicks have grown, they have learnt to turn themselves round, point their pink bottoms to the garage floor and push out their white blobs of excrement over the side of the nest. We have been surprised by the number of visits the parent birds make. The average has been about fifty visits an hour for about fourteen hours each day. The young take around twenty-one days to fledge, so that would mean some 15,000 mouthfuls of squashed flies, before the young fly the nest.

Our first swim in the sea this year was at Bantham, last week. The summer holidays have arrived and the beach was well scattered with families, sun bathing, making sand castles and playing cricket. Between the yellow and red flags, far out by the sea's edge, were the hardy bathers. We left our clothes by the low cliffs of The Ham and gave a glance up to the cliff-top. For over a hundred years there was a sand martin colony here. The soft 'head', above the solid rock, was ideal for excavating their nest holes. When numbers decreased, following the drought and famines in their wintering grounds south of the Sahara, the colony failed. For ten years there have been no nesting pairs at Bantham.

We walked down the ripple-ridged sand towards the sea. There were occasional curls of lugworm casts. As we reached the sea, a low, friendly surf lapped about our ankles. The shallows had been warmed by the sun, which cast a golden net of light over the shadowed sea bed. Children towing surf boards were high-stepping over the waves. Mum and dad looked on with smiles of far away happiness; seeing themselves twenty years ago. We plunged in and swam through the breakers out into the cold, deeper water and soon came, shivering back again.

As we returned, we walked through the shallow, almost tepid pools left from the last tide. There we found shrimps, not transparent like the prawns but grey, speckled with buff, white, black and amber. They matched the sand exactly. As we watched, they shuffled their pale legs and disappeared into the sand.

July 12th 1999

For seven weeks we have been watching a pair of great crested grebes on Slapton Ley. Their nest was a raft of reed and rush stems, anchored around a few stems of old reed-mace. On 25th May, Bryan Ashby and I witnessed the pair using the raft as a marriage bed, mating three times within ten minutes.

On 31st May an easterly wind had whipped up wavelets across the ley and they were washing right over the nest. But by the next day the birds were back. On 3rd June Chris Pierce and I walked down into the reeds, carrying armfuls of angle-iron. We walked stealthily out through the reeds, which swayed above our heads. The water rose above our ankles, to our knees and, by the time we stood behind the final fringe of reeds, we were nearly up to our waists in water. Here we pushed in the metal stakes and bolted on the cross-pieces to make a framework for the hide. The grebe sat on the nest, undisturbed, throughout.

When the hide was in place, we had cut a narrow gap in the reeds so that we had an uninterrupted view of the grebe on the nest. We took it in turns, Bryan, Chris and I, to sit in the hide and watch the bird, only ten yards away. We felt we could stroke her silky white neck and breast. Her black, forked crest was iridescent in the sunshine. The ruff around her neck was rich chestnut. From the base of her thin, steel-grey bill a black line led to the vermilion eye, set in a pure white face.

Great crested grebes at their nest.

The male appeared, surfacing among the lily pads. The female stood up, revealing three, dirty white eggs, long and oval. She waddled to the edge of the nest, lobed feet splayed wide, and tobogganed into the water. He jumped onto the nest, straddled the eggs and rearranged them with his bill, before settling down.

On 20th June we found the water level had dropped and the lesser reed-mace around the nest had grown up and screened the sitting bird from the hide. So I stripped down to my under-pants, crept out through the reeds and submerged. Shoals of fish-fry swam about me as I floated towards the nest with only my head showing above the water. The parent slipped off the nest as I approached. Quietly I removed the few leaves that obscured the view, as Chris whispered instructions from the hide. Within moments I was slipping back the way I had come. Soon the grebe returned, seemingly little concerned by the intrusion of the bald-headed 'bird' – perhaps a strange variety of coot.

Bryan and Chris took some lovely photographs of the birds on the nest and changing over, during the next few days. We spent hours watching them. The flowers of the white water-lilies came out and spread, like poached eggs, among the rounded leaves. Sometimes one of the pair would open its beak, as if yawning, showing a pink gape and tongue. Sometimes the grebe would bury her beak in her soft grey and salmon-pink flanks and appear to go to sleep.

When Chris was in the hide on the afternoon of 30th June the grebe stretched its neck upright, fanned out its ruff, Elizabethan style, and grunted in alarm. The cause of the trouble was a pair of moorhens, which appeared paddling and squabbling through the reeds close to the nest. Chris rapidly fired off several shots with the camera. Not until the pictures were developed did we realise that one of the eggs had hatched and a chick was peeping out from under the soft, grey shoulder feathers of the worried parent. When Chris returned the next day he saw a scrawny white and black-striped neck emerge from under the sitting bird's wings – the day-old chick climbed onto its mother's back and hid under a feather duvet. The male bird arrived with a downy feather in his bill, which he had plucked from his own breast. He reached over and gave it to the chick, which ate it greedily. Father swam off and pulled another feather from his breast. This time he gave it to his wife, who passed it over her shoulder to the reptilian nestling. The next day we all saw the same fascinating form of breast feeding and by then there were two chicks hatched. On the morning of 3rd July, Bryan and Cecelia James saw the birds by the nest for the last time. The two young were perched on the parent's back, as she swam down the edge of the island of water-lilies and out into the ley.

July 20th 1999

The natural world has slipped into fifth gear and we have reached the lazy plateau of high summer. The holidays have arrived, the grasses, like the nodding barley, are turning a tawny gold. In the hedgerows the silvery spires of mugwort have replaced the purple foxgloves.

Gatekeeper butterflies, orange and brown, are fluttering around the rosy petals of the bramble flowers and the larger, meadow brown butterflies rise lazily from the bleached meadows.

Barbara has had me swimming in the sea and lying on a sun-soaked beach to recover. Despite the coldness of the water, swimming over the waving forest of fingered kelp is a wonderful, other-worldly experience – the seaweeds are like the arms of olive-skinned giants performing a continuous, graceful Mexican wave.

At the edge of the old road above Leasfoot Beach at Thurlestone, the prickly, blue-flowered sea holly is in blossom; it is a relative of the garden eryngos. Bumble bees always seem attracted by the sea holly and many white-tailed and red-tailed bumble bees were buzzing around the globes of flower.

In the sandy grassland behind the sea holly was a fine stand of greater knapweed, that tall, purple-rayed relative of hardheads. Creeping along the ground was sea bindweed and the pretty, yellow-flowered ladies' bedstraw. The common hedge bedstraw is now out in most of our hedge banks, veiling whole stretches in speckled white. The insects of Thurlestone have been busy pollinating the tiny flowers. Next to the ladies' bedstraw were other bedstraw plants with paler yellow flowers. These were fertile hybrids between the two bedstraws. The insects had brought pollen from the hedge bedstraw and then visited the ladies' bedstraw, which had produced a new variety of seed – one of nature's genetic modifications.

Thanks to the kindness of friends, I have been on two magical boat trips this week, one from Bantham to Aveton Gifford and one around the Kingsbridge and Salcombe Estuary to do our monthly bird count. We found four broods of baby shelduck, all reduced to only two or three survivors. The little egrets are back in full force from Brittany and Normandy; there were six on the Avon and about thirty roosting in the waterside trees near Lincombe.

Insects are also migrants. Gordon Wainright had the good fortune to see a death's head hawk moth fly in off the sea and settle on the rocks, while he was fishing near Bigbury. He even managed to photograph it. I put out the moth trap this week and the catch included six poplar hawk moths but no death's heads.

View over Bantham.

July 2nd 2001

It's amazing what you can see from a tractor-cab. Roger Hosking was driving the tractor on their farm in Modbury, when he saw a buzzard flop down by the hedge. The white scuts of several rabbits shot away into their burrows but one rabbit remained, clamped in the buzzard's talons. It screamed, as only rabbits can. Then, out from the hedge bank appeared the rufous head and long whiskers of a fox; he strolled forward. The buzzard lifted its head, raised its wings in alarm

41

and jumped into the air, releasing the rabbit from its yellow talons as it did so. He flapped up into an oak tree in the hedge. The fox sauntered up to claim his second-hand breakfast but the startled rabbit shook himself and darted away down the nearest burrow. Roger had a new sequence to add to his fifty years of wildlife photography – the one that got away.

At the end of June we had an idyllic day near New Bridge, on the Dart – a butterfly day. We walked under the mossy-arched bridge, where the sunlight filtered through the leaves and rippled over the peat-brown river bed. A grey wagtail flew off, yellow belly flashing like another patch of sunlight. Out along the path to Deeper Marsh we passed the alder buckthorn bushes, which are the food plant for brimstone butterfly caterpillars. Soon we saw our first brimstone – a bright yellow male – followed by several more, including the almost white females. When they alight they close their wings, resembling two overlapping, pointed leaves.

In the afternoon we walked down Dr Blackall's Drive, from the top of the hill between New Bridge and Poundsgate. On some gorse bushes, sheltered by a granite wall, we found a colony of green hairstreak butterflies. About six males were perched on the spiky tips, basking in the sun. They too always settle with their wings closed, showing a grass-green camouflage. We only see the butterflies from the end of April to the beginning of July. Their caterpillars pupate in August and remain in the ground as little, brown pupae, tended by ants - their nannies until next April or May, when they emerge as butterflies.

This week, above Maceley Cove, we had some grandstand views of dark green fritillary butterflies, their black-veined, orange wings stretched out, or folded up showing the underwing flushed with green. They sipped nectar from the gaudy, purple flowers of greater knapweed, by the path. As we stood looking down at the sandy cove and rugged promontary of Gammon Head, we admired the mass of bloody cranesbill in flower round the cliff-edge.

The night shift, when most of the moths emerge, has been busy during these humid nights. Brown moths with black marks – heart and darts – are the most common at present, closely followed by two fluffy-headed moths – the white and buff ermines.

August 25th 1998

We made a pilgrimage last week, to a chapel on Dartmoor, beside the rounded hill of Huntingdon Warren. On the hillside we could see the losenge-shaped mounds where the rabbits made their burrows and the warrener netted or snared them. The remains of the warrener's cottage was there by the stream. Upstream from the ruin we found the chapel, in a grassy dell with a low wall of stones at one end. At the east end were three granite steps, nearly covered with grass and yellow-flowered tormentil. Above them stood an upright stone, only two or three feet high. A grey crust of lichen almost covered it but clearly visible, deeply incised, was a cross.

At Keble Martin's Chapel, with his autobiography and Concise Flora.

This was what we had come to see. It was where the five sons of the vicar of Dartington, Charles Martin, and some of their cousins came every year from 1904 to 1914, to spend a week camping. They had carved the cross into the stone and set up this dell as their chapel. One of the young men was Keble Martin, a clergyman like his father. They used to collect milk and eggs every day from the warrener's cottage. Once they baptised the latest baby for the warrener and his wife. The three oldest children used to walk the four miles over the moor to school at Holne each day.

The Martin family dammed the stream to make a bathing pool and caught trout for their breakfast. Keble Martin records how he drew pictures of bilberry, soft rush, bell heather and ling. These were later coloured and form part of his *Concise British Flora in Colour,* which was published over fifty years later in 1965.

Keble Martin devoted his life to work as a parish priest; very much a life of service. However he would snatch a few days between Sundays to travel over Britain finding and drawing flowers to complete his project to illustrate Britain's flora. He also found time to edit the *Devon Flora*, produced in 1939. Keble Martin was nearly ninety when his life's work was at last published. It gave him such pleasure. The book topped the bestseller list for months. It is a classic. He received many honours and, although a humble man, he delighted in them.

We took my cousin, also a lover of the countryside and the clergyman son of a clergyman father, to see the chapel. We started at Shipley Bridge and walked up the road towards the Avon Dam. Here we skirted the old quarry and the reservoir and followed the course of the Avon, along the Abbot's Way to Huntingdon Cross. At the cross we turned right and walked northwards by the peaty stream of the Wella Brook past tin workings and the ruins of the warrener's cottage and imagined the Martin family, with their handcart loaded with tents and provisions arriving at the same spot, nearly a hundred years ago.

Meanwhile back on the Kingsbridge Estuary the birds are gathering. Robert Pearce, on the evening cruise of the River Maid, reports over fifty little egrets roosting near Lincombe. David Amas and Michael Brooking have seen parties of migrant waders - dunlin, ringed plover and a few little stint and sanderling, sitting exhausted along the tide line.

August 20th 2001

Clara was only four but she was the star of our natural history outing to Beesands. About thirty of us went on one of the South Hams District Council's 'Coast and Countryside' walks, looking for flowers and the mini-beasts that live amongst them. Whatever we were hunting, Clara seemed to always find it first, or find something else and show us that instead. Everyone helped to make sure Clara's enthusiasm was not squashed, for it is a precious gift.

In the grassland behind the shingle ridge at Beesands we found hundreds of grasshoppers, many ladybirds and other beetles, including the orange soldier beetles. On a plant of ragwort we found the yellow and black striped caterpillars of the cinnabar moth. Taking nectar from the thistle flowers and spreading their wings were beautiful small tortoiseshell butterflies. Nibbling at the prickly leaves of the thistles we found tortoise beetle larvae, which look like tiny, dirty-green hedgehogs covered by black crumbs of their own excreta – a novel form of camouflage. The adults could be mistaken for green ladybirds or miniature tortoises.

By Widdicombe Ley black-tailed skimmers, steel-blue dragonflies flew low over the water and Valerie Belsey, one of our leaders, pointed out one settled right beside us. On our way back, through the longer grass we made our best discovery. We had spread out, looking for more insects, when Ella Constantine came up cradling a big caterpillar. The two pairs of pretend eyes on the side of the head showed it to be the offspring of some kind of elephant hawk-moth but unlike the normal elephant hawk-moth it had no horn at the tail-end. It was also smaller and greyer than those we find feeding on rose-bay willow-herb or our fuschia bushes. Ella had found the caterpillar of the much rarer small elephant hawk-moth, which feeds on the leaves of ladies' bedstraw. This low-growing, yellow flowered plant is common at Beesands and at all our coastal shingle banks and sand dunes. The crushed sea shells provide the calcium the plant needs for it is a typical plant of chalk and limestone hills. For all of us this was our first small elephant hawk-moth caterpillar; thank you Ella.

A few days before, I had put the moth trap on for National Moth Night. When I went to see what had flown in, after an overcast and muggy night, I was amazed to find more than two hundred moths resting under the old egg cartons on the floor of the trap. 102 of these were one species - the flame shoulder. Altogether there were forty different species in the catch but no elephant hawk-moths.

Last Saturday the Watch Club visited Horsley Cove, near Prawle, to go rock-pooling with Sally and Alice Henderson. In no time Alistair Parsons had netted a bowlful of prawns. Zak Clarke caught the first fish; a Montagu's blenny – named after George Montagu, who lived in Kingsbridge. It had a greeny-brown body with blue spots. Gabby Clarke and Alice soon caught more fish – five-bearded rocklings, a fatherlasher and several fifteen-spined sticklebacks. Like the freshwater, three-spined stickleback they flicker their pectoral fins like a pair of fans. Under the stones, which we carefully replaced, we found not only shore crabs but fiddler, edible and broad-clawed porcelain crabs too. On the beach, before we left, Gabby found a cowrie shell. This one had no spots; it was *Trivia arctica* a type of cowrie that George Montagu had been one of the first to identify. What a rich variety of life we have in the South Hams – however small or ugly, no species is trivial, every species has its part to play, especially us.

August 15th 2006

A Jersey tiger was resting on the wall of one of the new houses in Montagu

Close, at the top of Kingsbridge Fore Street, its cream and black stripes blending with the cream paint. This tiger was not a dangerous mammal but a harmless moth. It seemed to be appropriate for it to be resting within yards of where George Montagu lived, from 1798 to 1815, for it was Montagu's love-child Henry D'Orville who first found the Jersey tiger moth in Devon.

Jersey tiger on sea aster.

Henry D'Orville's mother was Eliza D'Orville, who lived with George Montagu, as his 'friend in science' in what was then known as Knowle Cottage or just The Knowle – now Prospect House, I believe. At 9.00p.m. on 14th August 1871, in a garden in Exeter, he captured this striking moth on tansy flowers, which he had painted with liquid sugar. Henry D'Orville had become curator of Exeter Museum, a post for which he was well-qualified having known his father's museum in Knowle Cottage, full of stuffed birds, seashells and strange antiquities.

As a boy, he would have helped his father go fishing, dig for worms in the estuary and tend the birds in the aviaries and on the big pond. He would have watched his mother meticulously drawing what Montagu had procured, dead or alive, from shellfish and shrimps to birds and bats. Henry, Montagu's natural son, chose moths as a special study.

Two years later two were seen at Hazelwood, near Loddiswell. South Devon, between Exeter and Plymouth, has remained its mainland stronghold and it has become quite common. I have seen more Jersey tigers than small tortoiseshell butterflies this summer. Pam Waitling, in Chillington, had five in her garden last week. In Britain, outside Devon and its neighbouring counties, it has been very rare but in the last few years has begun to expand dramatically – being found as far east as London. On the continent and in the Channel Islands it is common but nearly always has red underwings, while our colonies have evolved mostly yellow or orange underwings, during their century and a half of evolution as a British species. Perhaps we should call it D'Orville's tiger.

Whilst walking in Fernworthy Forest last week, Peter Cummings and a group of South Hams ramblers he was leading came to a sudden halt. Down from the conifers flew a pair of crossbills to settle only ten yards away from them on a grassy ride — like fat, red sparrows with crossed scissor-blades bills. Later they had stunning views of that beautiful butterfly, the silver-washed fritillary.

The Lobelia counters in Andrew's Wood also saw a silver-washed fritillary, big and orange, basking in the sun, and twelve other species of butterfly. The nine of us spread across each of the clearings in turn and moved slowly forward, recording every heath lobelia plant. The three ponies, now grazing in the Two Andrews' Clearing, galloped up to see what we were doing. After five hours of counting, we finished with a total of 2,694 plants. Over the thirty-two years we have been making an annual count, the numbers have fluctuated wildly but this year's total is virtually the same as the first count back in 1975.

August 29th 2006

I am not going to use my old trainers any more; they will stay on the garage floor. I have found a toad hiding in them. On each occasion I feel gently into the toe, the toad is still there, so I have decided to leave him or her undisturbed. Most days he is in residence, sometimes in the left, sometimes in the right shoe. When I check at bedtime I have sometimes seen him in the garage – fat, brown and warty. Toads can live to forty years of age.

During the lobelia count at Andrew's Wood in Aspen Clearing, where we had our lunch, both emperor and golden-ringed dragonflies were active, chasing other insects or chasing each other when their territories were invaded. Some thistle-down floated across the clearing and a big, blue emperor dragonfly mistook it for some tasty item of prey and repeatedly closed in on it for the kill.

At Staverton railway station, an elephant had a narrow escape. As we waited for the steam train to arrive, I was looking at the flowers growing along the fence. They were a butterfly's paradise – pink hemp-agrimony, yellow fleabane and sweet-scented, purple buddleia. In the chippings either side of the line was a forest of horsetails; we had seen their golden-brown stems topped by spore-filled

Elephant hawk-moth.

Staverton Station.

cones in the spring. Between the sleepers was some pale toadflax, a straggling plant with pale lilac flowers, which is not common in the South Hams. As I looked down, I heard the whistle of the train approaching. Then I saw the elephant.

If it had not moved I wouldn't have seen it, for it was well camouflaged, browny-grey like the chippings. It stretched out its head, extending it just like an elephant's trunk. Six small legs gripped the chippings and hauled the body forwards. This strange creature was a caterpillar, about three inches long, looking for some loose soil in which to bury itself and pupate. Not until next May or June would it emerge, as a beautiful pink and green elephant hawk-moth. The caterpillar was half way across the track when the train arrived, hissing steam and belching smoke. The train driver never saw the elephant crawling under his green dragon!

Many banks and verges are speckled yellow with late summer 'dandelions'. The two most common have no leaves up the stems, just a few bracts like little cats' ears. They both have rosettes of dandelion-like leaves, around the base of the stem. The bigger one is catsear. Catsear leaves have rounded lobes and are very hairy. The smaller one is autumn hawkbit, now at the height of its flowering season. It is not hairy and its rosette leaves are sharply lobed and pointed at the ends. Another species has small, arrow-shaped leaves up the stem and they hug the stem; this is smooth hawksbeard. All these species prefer open grassy habitats. On shadier banks, the leafy hawkweed, which has oval, pointed leaves all the way up the stem, is coming into flower. Especially by paths and lanes by the sea, is a dandelion-like plant with rough prickly leaves; this is called prickly ox-tongue on account of it feeling similar to the rasp of a bullock's tongue on your skin. So the late summer 'dents de lions' are different animals – a fascinating tribe of 'cats', 'hawks' and 'oxen'.

September 14th 1999

The signs of autumn are all around us; hips and haws are colouring the hedgerows, the robins are giving their watery, autumn songs and Barbara is picking blackberries. We are over half way to our annual target of twenty pounds and I expect Alan O'Shaughnessy has already reached that. The ivy blossom is out too and there is an influx of insects. There are plenty of hoverflies and red admiral butterflies around the ivy. While I was swimming off Yarmer beach, at Thurlestone, several red admirals flew in from over the sea. Insect immigration has been noticeable, with silver-Y moths hovering round the late flowers. Even on the salt marshes there have been silver-Ys feeding at the yellow and mauve sea aster flowers. This week another migrant, a humming bird hawk-moth, gave us a demonstration of perfect hovering; it stopped in front of a red valerian bloom, its grey and chestnut wings a blur of movement but its body absolutely stationary. It extended its long tongue to feed on the nectar deep down the corolla tube of the flower.

Red admiral.

In Modbury, Derek Wilkinson has found five elephant hawk-moth caterpillars – one of our resident hawk-moths – on a bush in his garden. This is the time to look out for them, especially on fuschia or rose-bay willow-herb. They are quite frightening, as they swell up their heads, expanding their four, false eyes and extending their elephant's trunk nose.

We took a trip on the River Maid, and like all our outings with Peter Moule and Robert Pearce, it was a memorable occasion. We left the Crabshell Inn, Kingsbridge, and almost immediately saw a dozen little egrets, perched in the oak trees round Park Bay. It is ten years since the egrets began their annual immigrations from France and they are now resident for most of the year.*

Following the snaking channel, we passed Sandwich terns sitting on the marker posts and buoys so close that we could see the yellow tips to their black bills. In Widegates, Robert pointed to a long line of birds along Charleton Bay. Peter took the River Maid gliding very slowly towards them. There were over three hundred curlew by the water's edge, some alert, stretching upwards, some apparently asleep, with their curved beaks hidden under their wings. Many were carrying on a muted conversation in fluting, throaty tones. About a hundred and fifty black and white oystercatchers were packed in at one end. There were groups of dunlin and ringed plover. We admired their plumage in the rich, evening sunlight. Eventually the birds took flight — sheer beauty.

We continued down through The Bag to Salcombe, over The Bar, past the jagged rocks above Starehole Bay and out into the gently rocking sea. We sat looking westwards, where the afterglow of the sunset was reflected in the swell. A fulmar, our equivalent to an albatross, swept over us on stiff wings, dipping towards the pastel-coloured sea. Fulmars have spread dramatically southwards from the north of Scotland. The first South Devon bird was seen off Bolt Head in 1946; fifty years have passed and now they are an elegant commonplace.

*They began nesting on the estuary in 2004. Twenty pairs now breed.

September 16th 2002

Last week-end the Devon Association's botanical group had been given permission to walk down the Flete Estate carriageway, by the River Erme. At 8.00a.m. the tide was brimming, the valley sides, clothed in dark green and yellowing oak woods, were reflected in the still water. Spikes of spartina grass and sea aster from the saltmarshes, poked up from the water and green sheets of sea lettuce, washed up on the tide from Wonwell beach, were caught on them, like flags. A party of wigeon dabbled on the tide and one whistled, announcing they are back in their winter home.

Our botanical walk began here, by the carriageway, where a clump of our native golden-rod was in flower on the bank. We walked along the road, under the oaks of Holbeton Wood. More knopper galls than acorns were scattered on the tarmac. Knopper galls seem abundant this year, sticky, grooved lumps on stalks, where the acorns should be. Galls are growths produced by plants, usually around where a gall-midge or gall-wasp has laid its eggs. The oak tree is host to more than a dozen kinds of gall-wasp – pea galls and spangle galls on the back of its leaves, artichoke and marble galls on the twigs. Knopper galls arrived in Britain about thirty years ago. Disaster was predicted for the acorn crop but the oak trees still produce acorns enough to produce new seedlings and to feed the jays and squirrels.

At Efford House, we stopped at the edge of the wood and admired the views down the estuary and across the salt-marsh. Growing by the trackway was a bank of pencilled cranesbill and, opposite it, a mass of giant golden-rod, both originally garden escapes. While we were looking down at these, Roger Smith was looking up into the blue sky – "Peregine!" he cried.

Wheeling above us was a creamy-breasted peregrine, its dark moustaches clearly showing. With it was a sparrow-hawk, with barred underparts and rounded wings, and three buzzards all soaring on the same thermal. "We only need an osprey to make it perfect," I said.

Below Efford House, where the public footpath from Holbeton gives access to the riverside carriageway for a hundred yards, we stopped to explore the flora of the salt-marsh. We sat there and enjoyed our picnic lunch. Out on the mud-flats were gulls, oystercatchers and a few dozen dunlin, busily probing in the mud along the water's edge. Suddenly they all took flight.

"An osprey! An osprey!" shouted some of the group. They had seen it plunge into the river. Now the rest of us saw it, flying low and with difficulty up towards Clyng Mill. From one, long-legged talon hung a huge silver fish. It disappeared behind the oak wood and reappeared some minutes later, far away against blue sky and towering cumulus clouds but with the fish still shining in the sunlight.

September 1st 2003

The goldfinch landed on my head. Dusk was fast approaching. I had looked up while walking under a birch tree, because of a repeated, twittering call. The bird had flown onto my sparsely covered scalp, still twittering. It moved down onto my left shoulder and fluttered onto my right. I stayed absolutely still and then slowly raised my hand to my shoulder. The goldfinch hopped onto my outstretched fingers. I lowered my hand and saw a small, brown bird; the head was browny-grey but the stubby wings had a gold bar and black tips. This was a young goldfinch not long out of the nest – a very late brood. Country folk used to call young goldfinches 'grey-pates', before their heads developed the bands of red, white and black. There were more twitterings from high in the birch tree. Had the fledgling mistaken me, bald-pate, for its parent? I gently lifted it back into the branches but it flew down again onto my head.

I was going down the garden to take some hedge trimmings to the compost heap and four times I passed under the birch tree and each time the goldfinch came twittering onto my head or shoulder. It worried me that I might be distracting the bird from his real parents, so the last time I passed I kept moving. Something brushed my knee and, looking down, I saw the goldfinch had fluttered to keep up with me and had crash-landed into the grass. I took him on my hand. He kept his balance by waving his short, black and white tail. I stood under the tree like a falconer, with a miniature hawk on my hand. After that I kept away, hoping the parents would return to it. The next day a party of goldfinches flew over and I hoped my adopted fledgling was one of them.

On Tuesday, Helen and Josh Hibbard and Olive Maddock joined me on a rainy morning to finish this year's lobelia count in Andrew's Wood. We saw a charm of goldfinches on the seed-heads of some tall marsh thistles; about a hundred bounced off into the drizzly air. The golden wing stripes showing up despite the murky conditions. Many of them were grey-pates.

The butterfly and moth bananza has continued. On willow trees in Michael and Mel Baker's garden, at Osborne Newton Cottages, were more than thirty red admiral butterflies and scores of wasps and hoverflies. The attraction was the wet, sweet honeydew from massed patches of blackfly gathered for an autumn 'love-in' on the willow branches. Even aphids have their place in the web of life. In July, Michael Baker had photographed a privet hawk-moth in their garden.

Through the post I received photos of two convolvulus hawk-moths, one from Claire Drinkwater's patio at South Milton and the other of a dark specimen from Ann Borne at Salcombe.

The abundance of butterflies has reminded David Balkwill of Aveton Gifford of the summer of 1948, when there were a host of butterflies feasting on the fallen fruit beneath some old pear trees. A Polish man, Tadeusz, was working on their farm. He was a keen lepidopterist and took photos of the butterflies. They were so drunk on the rotting pears they could not fly away and he was able to take some wonderful snapshots. Tadeusz had escaped from a Russian prison camp by swimming the River Volga, made his way to Britain and fought bravely in the Polish Air Force during the Second World War.

September 20th 2004

An egret flew over Charleton seawall, as Jane Rogers declared 'The Chris Rogers Memorial Hide' open, to a crowd of well-wishers including all the children at Charleton School. We stood in the autumn sunshine. What a beautiful day for a wonderful occasion. As I arrived, two kingfishers had flown down the reed-fringed dyke in tandem, their blue slipstreams overlapping, swinging from side to side. The hide is a real community achievement. Thanks were given to those who dreamed of it, planned it, paid for it and finally built it. Quietly, in the background, four men ensured that the opening day was such a success: Jim Bennett, Des Lamble, Paul Rogers and Tony Tabb. They were almost invisible on the day. They have worked hours on the hide, putting the important finishing touches, painting, pinning up identification charts, bringing down chairs and giving lifts to the less able. At the opening ceremony they stood unobtrusively at the back.

Charleton Marsh.

Wal Towler spoke of his dream having come true. Nigel Mortimer spoke of the unsung wildlife heroes of the estuary, such as diatoms, creatures often invisible to the eye. Without them the stars, like the osprey or the otter, would not be here. From the hide we can look out over the marsh, with its reed-beds and shallow pools, and in the other direction over the wide expanse of the estuary as the tide rises and falls. It will give pleasure and understanding to many people, old and young, for many years to come.

On Saturday afternoon we were at another of my favourite places – walking round Andrew's Wood with a Devon Wildlife Trust group. They were good at finding hidden gems. One appeared, uncannily, on cue. We were standing by some rose-bay willow-herb and I was explaining that it is a food plant of the elephant hawk-moth caterpillar, when one of the group spotted one of the caterpillars crawling at our feet; grey-brown, with two false eyes on either side of its head and a curved spike on the tail end. Soon after we stopped by a fence and watched several common darter dragonflies settled on the sun-warmed wooden bars. They are autumn dragonflies; the males with red bodies and the females with golden-brown. Two girls, Aisha and Anastasia crept to within a yard of one of them, while another almost landed on their heads, hovering over them like a helicopter. On the gate-post nearby, Bruce Church found young lizards; dark brown dinosaurs only three inches long, basking in the sun. That evening it was back to the estuary for a cruise with the Methodist Church.

We had an exciting boat trip, with close views of all the common waders, including about thirty oystercatchers roosting on some old pontoons in The Bag. The highlight came when Peter Moule spotted a bird perched on a dead branch in the wood at Heath Point. Was it a heron or was it an osprey? We were looking into the setting sun and it was difficult to see. A heron flew up – a sigh of disappointment – and then another big bird flew out of the tree and away into the blaze of the sun. At last it flew out of the dazzle and we could see its long, feather-fingered wings, the white underparts and neck and the black stripe through the eye. As the osprey made a great circle over the mouth of Blanksmill and Collapit Creeks, we watched, spellbound.

OCTOBER

October 6th 1997

Look up to the moor and for some weeks now the dark green bracken has been turning rusty brown. It started as a rim along the upper edge, below Ugborough Beacon, and has worked down, like a falling tide, recording the approach of autumn. This week we were on Dartmoor, following the Glaze Brook northwards. Barbara, looking ahead, saw a large, dark thrush take off from a berry-laden rowan tree. "What was that?" she asked.

I was too busy looking down at the path, where red darter dragonflies and red admiral butterflies were settling on the sun-warmed stones. We stopped and there, sitting under a thorn bush, surrounded by the green and rusty bracken were Terry and Judy Hockin, who had been silently waiting and watching for three hours. They had seen a ring ouzel fly into the rowan tree and begin to feed on the bright orange berries. Terry focussed his video camera and had been filming when we, 'clumping two-boots' frightened the bird away.

Terry rewound the video for us to see the pictures he had taken. As we stood, a redstart flew into the neighbouring thorn bush and sat in its gnarled branches, its red tail quivering. Terry had seen two earlier and filmed them. The ring ouzel then returned; first to a distant thorn and finally back into the rowan tree. We saw the new-moon necklace of white on his black chest and the pale edging to the dark wings as he ripped off the berries. We had been given a lesson in patience and had our reward. Wait and the wildlife will come to you.

This week has been the last for picking blackberries. It is past October 1st, so the Devil will have spat, or worse, on them. In trying to reach our annual target of 20lbs., we have disturbed scuttling, brown shield bugs and butterflies from the berries. Most of the butterflies have been red admirals, velvet-brown and black, with red and white beauty spots on their wing-tips. We have seen a few commas – gorgeous, rich orange as they fly. The underside is the russet-brown of a crinkled bramble leaf; the camouflage is perfect, except for six spindly, white legs protruding and the neat, white comma mark in the centre of the wing.

With the scent of ripe blackberries, we have also had the musty, honeyed perfume of ivy blossom. Blackberry fruit and ivy blossom provide a hedgerow harvest festival for the insects. Ivy is the last, abundant flower of the year. Around the blossoms swarm the bees and wasps, flies, hoverflies and butterflies, all eager for their last feast.

As the sun goes down and we go to bed, the night shift begins. The night-flying, autumn moths feed on the ivy and blackberries too. Their subtle, autumn colours are beautiful. I shall go out now and switch on the moth trap.

October 1st 2001

Everywhere craneflies, long legs dangling, have been weakly flying, like rudderless microlights . These insects are always abundant in autumn. They have only one pair of wings. The hind pair have evolved into drumsticks, called halteres, which act as gyroscopes, keeping a sense of balance as the cranefly makes its uncertain way. The males have a rounded tip to the abdomen. The females have a pointed tip, their ovipositor, with which they lay their eggs into the soil. The eggs hatch into grey, leatherjacket grubs, which eat the roots of our crops. The flocks of rooks, poking in the stubble and ploughed fields, consume thousands.

September has been a month of brisk winds, impressive cloudscapes and fickle, sunny days – good for our late holiday-makers.

One morning, early, I went down to Frogmore to survey the patches of saltmarsh, which Nigel Mortimer and I had measured two years ago. At Cleavehouse Bay a few mauve stars of sea aster were still in flower. Along the foreshore, the soft, estuary mud was spottled with green and brown acorns, fallen from the overhanging oak trees. A pair of jays screeched from up in the tree-tops, collecting acorns to eat and to store, and flew off, with their distinctive, jerkily undulating flight, each holding an acorn or six in its beak.

In the yellowing, Dart Valley oaks above Holne Bridge there were jays too. We went there, inspired by the talk on the Dartmoor Dart that Geoffrey Weymouth had given us at the Kingsbridge Natural History Society. We stood on Holne Bridge and looked downstream. The gold and green leaves and tree trunks like cathedral pillars made a perfect picture of autumn. Above the bridge were two female goosanders, perched on boulders, taking a rest from fishing. Behind them, a dipper was busily hopping into the water, submerging and popping up, like a cork, and bobbing us a curtsey from a water-ringed boulder.

The 29th September was 'the last day of summer' and we walked up the River Avon from Shipley Bridge. Jays were in the oaks near the car park and we disturbed a nuthatch scuffling for nuts and grubs in the leaf litter. He climbed up the trunk of a tall larch tree, Barbara following him in her binoculars until he was gone.

In a small quarry by the road and winding river, a party of six ring ouzels were feasting on the orange rowan berries. We feasted our eyes on their beautifully scalloped breasts and white-edged flight feathers. Our sunny, autumn walk finished at the little waterfalls, by the last curve of the river before the dam. Below the falls was a deep, dark pool where a few trout cruised just below the surface. A cranefly made its uncertain way over the pool, in the sunshine. One of the fish leapt right out of the water with a 'plop'; the cranefly continued its flight. The fish leapt again and this time the cranefly was gone.

October 25th 2004

It was a wild day. We watched the waves crashing on the sandy beach and flying spray shooting over the harbour wall at Hope Cove. Suddenly we realised that seals were cavorting in courtship dances, right below us at the edge of the sea. There seemed to be three of them, probably two bulls and a cow – although only one of them had the big, Roman nose of a fully mature bull. He clambered onto the back of the cow and together they rolled over and over in the frothing waves. The other wrapped his body around them both, the whole mass writhing like obese eels in a bubble-bath. For ten minutes we were enthralled by the romantic ballet. They would swim out, submerge and disappear, for their bottle noses to reappear a hundred yards out across the harbour, playing water leap-frog and chasing each other back to the shore, where the coupling began again.

Atlantic grey seal with pup on Hope Cove Beach.

The story had begun there three weeks ago, when a cow seal had given birth to her white, woolly pup, on the beach by the slipway from the old Inner Hope lifeboat station. Usually they give birth at the back of sea-caves, such as those around Bolt Tail, or at the top of very remote beaches; it is most unusual for them to give birth in so public a place. The local people and wildlife charities have kept

58

watch, so that mother and pup have been safe from people and dogs. Generally we care much more for wild creatures than we did a century ago; then they might well have been clubbed to death.

About half of the 200,000 Atlantic grey seals in the world live around the shores of Britain. They are big animals, about six feet long — a bit less for cows and a bit more for bulls. The cows weigh over twenty stone and the bulls can be between thirty and fifty stone. If they were six foot humans they would be disastrously overweight but for their life in the cold seas they are perfectly adapted. On the land they are clumsy but in the sea, swift and graceful – svelte mermaids and mermen. The cows mature quicker – two years before the bulls – and live around thirty-five years, about ten years longer than bulls.

They give birth to their pup in the autumn, when the adults are in peak condition. The speed of their growth to independence is amazing. The pup suckles from its mother for only about eighteen days, growing from about thirty pounds at birth to about a hundred pounds – seven stone! Mother meanwhile becomes quite slim, loosing as much weight as her pup gains. She eats nothing for three weeks. After this, the mother deserts the pup and it has to fend for itself. Now the mating season begins; bull seals and young adults gather near the birthing areas and they have a party. There are games and some sex but no food. The bulls do not hunt during the six weeks of the mating season. Once a cow has mated, the fertilised egg inside her womb divides a few times and then floats in the uterus until about February. Only then does it implant into the uterus wall and begin its seven month gestation.

Later, in a wild wind, we walked around Bolt tail. Keeping well back from the cliff, we watched the white waves crash into Red Rot Cove and the spouts of water from the three blow-holes shoot into the air. A single gannet flew low over the water, battling with the wind.

October 24th 2006

Olga Steele looked out and saw an otter by their pond in Manor Park, chewing at a big, silver eel. A few days later she saw the otter again and this time crept up and photographed it, while it chewed its way through one of their goldfish. Otters, thank goodness, are on the increase. Olga and George Steele's pond may well be the one in which George Montagu used to keep wildfowl. In April 1806 he wrote to his friend Robert Anstice, 'I am going to contrive a duckery by enclosing a part of a pond I have in my pleasure ground, so that those (birds) who live chiefly on water may indulge themselves.' He kept ducks, geese, swans, a very tame cormorant and the first black stork to be recorded in Britain. Montagu was interested in many branches of natural history. Last week, while walking on the beach near Millbay, I came across a seashell, Montagu's carpet-shell (*Venerupis*

George Montagu's pond restored by George and Olga Steele.

pullustra), lying on the sand, among tubes of sand-mason worms. Perhaps Montagu first found it at Millbay. I walked on down to the water's edge, for it was low tide and I could see the eel-grass bed exposed; long strands, like thick, green hair of Salcombe mermaids, lying on the sand. By the eel-grass, something was crawling towards the sea. Was it a worm? I looked closer and was amazed to see it was a hop-dog. These caterpillars, the larvae of pale tussock moths, used to be a pest in the Kentish hop fields. This one was marching determinedly a few inches from the lapping, salt water – quite the wrong habitat. I picked it up and walked back across a hundred yards of sand to the top of the beach and put the caterpillar into the hedge. Why had it been trying to commit suicide?

We found another hop-dog in Andrew's Wood. The caterpillar was a beautiful specimen with yellow, 'tooth-brush' bristles on its back, black stripes between its segments and a pink tuft on its tail-end. Our tasks in Andrew's Wood were to clear birch and sallow scrub from Dragonfly Clearing and dig out the silted up pond. We were pleased to see a blue-green hawker dragonfly settle by the pond. Sue Kendall was having a cup of coffee, sitting in the lee of a gorse bush. Beside her was a wandering snail (that lives both in and out of water), a damsel-fly and a shiny frog – the stuff from which fairy tales are made!

The third hop-dog of the week was under an oak tree by West Alvington Wood, during our Watch Club fungus foray. The children found it, together with several oak boletus fungi in the grass and leaf-litter. The children were amazing at spotting fungi, especially after the games of exploration and discovery (some of it blindfold) that Fiona van Es and Sally Henderson had prepared for them. Biologists have put fungi in a kingdom of their own, separate from plants, animals, protozoa and bacteria. Fungi have many special relationships with plants, from trees to algae. In grassland the children found ink-caps and fairy rings and on dead bramble stems tiny, white *Marasmius*. From tree stumps, grew groups of fairies' bonnets and black and white wicks of candlesnuff. Sycamore is a special host for some fungi; on the leaves we found tar-spot fungus, on dead twigs the orange pin-heads of coral-spot and, growing up from a rotten, fallen branch, Laura Williams discovered a host of 'dead Moll's fingers' — black, club-shaped fungi.

Hop-dog, pale tussock moth caterpillar.

NOVEMBER

November 10th 1997

A week of storms has driven birds, dramatic clouds and lashing rain across the sky. A few days before, we walked round Start Point to Mattiscombe Sands. From the lighthouse road we saw two kestrels hovering into the strong, easterly wind. To the south of Start Point, the tidal race was turbulent with white horses, where conflicting currents meet. Four canoeists, in sea kayaks, were working down the coast towards 'the race'. We climbed over the rocky ridge, which leads down to Start Point like a dinosaur's jagged back, and found shelter.

We sat in the sun and began a sea-watch. About a thousand gulls sat on the rocks, in the lee of the point. Most of them were herring gulls but there were over three hundred great black-backs. Out to sea, two razorbills sped low over the waves. They passed the canoeists, who were paddling into the most turbulent part of the tidal race. The waves seemed to come from all directions and the kayaks were plunging into them. Safe in our sheltered sun-trap, we felt the excitement and danger of their challenge.

Another auk flew by them; it seemed browner and was probably a guillemot. Then one of the canoes was upsidedown. We saw the white underside of the kayak and the flailing paddle of the man beneath the waves, trying to right himself. Several times we saw him struggle half upright, only to fall back again. Above him flew a tight pack of five very dark duck — two were black, three brown with pale cheek patches. They were scoter. Quickly I turned back to the canoes. All four were the right way up but, as I watched, a large wave came sideways and another of the group had turned turtle. This time the capsized man had come right out of his canoe and was holding onto the upturned hull. He tried to climb back in but they were in the worst of the race and the seas were huge. Two of the canoeists began, carefully, to make their way towards the shore. The other canoeist stayed with the capsized man, keeping close by him but making no attempt to help him. We could see they were being swept rapidly further and further, south-eastwards out to sea.

A grey bird with a long neck flew over them. In a moment, my thoughts had left the drama and were following the bird, looking for distinguishing marks. The trailing edges of the wings were white, where they joined the body. This was a great crested grebe in winter plumage. When I looked back to the kayaks this time, there had been no miraculous recovery. They continued drifting further out and every time the man tried to climb back into his canoe, he was toppled over by the breaking waves. Was the situation as desperate as it looked? At last, when they were nearly a mile from the shore, they drifted into less severe water. His friend came alongside the capsized canoe and rested his paddle across the two craft. The capsized man crawled into his own kayak and they both began, slowly and avoiding the race, to paddle for the shore and their waiting companions.

November 2nd 1998

Ted Hughes started one of his poems in *Autumn Nature Notes* with 'Water-wobbling, blue-sky-puddled October...' October and, sadly, Ted Hughes are gone.

On the day he died we were walking between Torcross and Start Point. There was blue sky and blue reflected in the wind-wobbled water of the sea, ley and puddle. The rains of the last few weeks have filled Slapton Ley to the brim. Where the overflow tunnel emerges onto the beach, the water was pouring out in a torrent and rushing down the shingle to the sea. Chris Riley, from Slapton Field Centre, told me that the tunnel was driven through the solid rock by Cornish or Welsh miners in 1856. But for the overflow tunnel, Torcross would have been flooded.

We followed the tide-line, our boots scrunching and slipping in the shingle. Barbara found a large whelk shell washed up with the flotsam and jetsam of weed and rubbish. Inside was the dead body of its last owner – a hermit crab. In death it had turned pink, like its relative the lobster. The ragged claws, the jointed legs and eyes on stalks hung limply from the shell.

Before we reached Beesands, we passed the almost invisible entrance to Sunnydale Quarry. On the loose, slate spoil piled up against the cliff, tall mulleins and hundreds of grey-green leaf-rosettes of yellow-horned poppies were growing.

On Widdicombe Ley, coots and tufted and pochard ducks rode on the choppy water but the wigeon we had seen a few weeks ago had moved on. A pair of stonechats perched on the tall, dead stalks of sea raddish, flicking their tails. We saw three more pairs between there and Start Point.

At Hallsands five swallows flew past, perhaps waiting for the weather to settle before crossing the Channel. Ten long-tailed tits slipped from a thicket of elm and follow-my-leadered into the cherry plantation. Although the original trees look old and gnarled, young suckers are spreading at either side.

As we approached Start Point car park, we disturbed two very faded butterflies – a tortoiseshell and a painted lady – near the end of their lives. We went on to find shelter and a view of the point. Below a rocky outcrop we sat and had our picnic and looked out over the sea. Off Start Point, in the rough water, seven gannets were fishing, plunging into the waves.

On our return, we had nearly reached Beesands when, swiftly, a bank of cloud began to eat up the blue sky. In moments it was pouring with rain but the sun still shone. A double rainbow curved in brilliant arches from the beach out into the sea. We walked onto the shingle, to where the end of the rainbow seemed to rest. There we found not a crock of gold but a spike of that poisonous plant, henbane, its urn-shaped, death-dealing seed capsules in serried ranks up the stem.

Ted Hughes might have approved the black irony.

November 11th 2002

A trip to Sharpham is like visiting a secret kingdom, tucked away behind Ashprington. The road leads to a sheltered peninsula defined by a hairpin loop of the River Dart. The steep wooded slopes across the river, the neat lines of vines growing on the southern slope and the towering outcrop of volcanic rock, fit for Valhalla, all make it feel like a scene from the Rhineland.

Bryan and Jane Ashby took me for a walk around the Sharpham nature trail. The trail begins at the shop, where the home-grown wines and cheeses are for sale. The path passes near the fine mansion and down the ridge of the peninsula, with sloping pasture to the left and the vineyards down to the right. A huge Lucombe oak grows over the path. Because of its dark green foliage, we thought it was a holm oak until we stood beneath it and saw the leaves had jagged, saw edges, more like a Turkey oak. William Lucombe, from Exeter, introduced the Turkey oak to his nursery in 1735. One must have hybridised with cork oaks growing nearby for, when he planted out some of the acorns from his Turkey oaks in 1762, he noticed that one grew particularly vigorously and kept its leaves through the winter. He recognised it as a hybrid, began grafting its shoots onto Turkey oak rootstock and sold it successfully throughout the west country as ' the Lucombe oak'. Work on building Sharpham House began in 1770, so this specimen may be over two hundred years old. Lucombe himself died at the age of 102 and was buried in a coffin made from a Lucombe oak.

In the vineyard we found several young men picking the last of the grapes into big boxes. They offered us some grapes to taste, which were deliciously sweet.

We followed the path down between the vines to the riverside hedge and continued to a stone quay, a lovely picnic spot with views up and down the river. By a stile was a tall holly tree with a mass of red berries. A spindle bush, its sprays of green twigs hung with thousands of tiny pink lanterns, some opening to reveal the orange seeds within, festooned over an old lime kiln. Limestone and coal, landed at the quay, were burnt in layers, reduced to lime and spread on the fields to sweeten the soil in the eighteenth and nineteenth Centuries.

We continued to Sharpham Point. Redwings flew out of the hawthorn bushes and a red admiral butterfly fluttered around the ivy blossoms that climbed up into the bushes. Bryan stalked out over the grassy apron of saltmarsh to try to

Jane Ashby and a holly bush at Sharpham.

The River Dart passing Sharpham Quay.

photograph a party of oystercatchers and a curlew which had landed at the water's edge, where an egret and a heron were already patrolling. When we had almost completed the circuit of the peninsula, we stopped below the impressive outcrop of volcanic rock and looked across to Fleet Mill Quay, where the rotting hull of the old paddle steamer, Kingswear Castle, lies.

For lunch we headed down to Dittisham, to the Ferry Inn. There, on the concrete pier we found a pair of crows repeatedly flying up into the air, dropping something onto the pier and flying down to peck at it. We went closer and found dozens of broken mussel shells and shore crab claws and carapaces. The crows' method of breaking through their prey's protective armour had been very effective.

November 8th 2004

What a wonderful fungus foray we had with the young naturalists – Jasper, Tom and Peter, Francis and Rosie, Laura and Robert and Jessica – at Topsham Bridge. Like hounds on a truffle hunt, they scurried around under the hazel bushes and sycamore trees, where a footpath leads off from the parking space just before the bridge. On a scrubby elder bush were lots of pinky-brown ears, soft to the touch; Judas' ears, a fungus commonly found on elder. Every few moments came the call, "Come and see!"

Black clubs, an inch or two high, with white, pithy insides, were growing from a rotting twig. The next cry was for a group of giant clubs, about ten, dirty brown, blunt ended horns a foot tall — both types of earth tongues..

Continuing down the footpath, we crossed a stream and a stile and stood beneath a big beech tree. We found husks of beech nuts, curved up like spiky, three-cornered pixies' caps. There were lots of small, coffee-coloured fungi perfectly camouflaged among the fallen leaves – deceivers, a very common and variable woodland toadstool. Near the stile were a few similar fungi with a purple tinge – amethyst deceivers. At the base of the beech tree were two, pink-capped fungi with white gills and stem – beech *Russula*s. The children found them all,

In the field by the beech tree, Alice Henderson, the club's junior leader, led the children in the hawk and robin game. They chased each other and learnt about food-chains. Fungi are a vital part of every food-chain, recycling dead matter into new life. The main parts of their bodies, fine threads of mycelium, spread unseen through dead wood or soil. As we played the game, a sharp-eyed mum spotted a nuthatch scuttling along the high branches of the beech tree.

We returned to Topsham Bridge, pausing to play Pooh-sticks, and walked down the road. Mr Betts, outside his house by the river, told the children how he and his wife had seen a family of otters playing in the river at about midnight a few days before. Tom and Peter Ballantine told him of the otter which became trapped in their garage at Loddiswell last summer and how they had released it at Hatch Bridge, with an RSPCA officer. Perhaps it was one of the family playing in the river by moonlight.

As we walked back, the sharp-eyed mum and Alice saw a dipper shoot upstream under the bridge.

The grand finale was at Aveton Wood, a few hundred yards up the Loddiswell road from Topsham. On one side of the entry path are larches, their needles golden; larch is a deciduous conifer. Beneath them the children found bright yellow toadstools, with a spongy texture beneath the cap, not gills. In the book it showed them exactly, complete with a spray of larch; they were larch *Boletus*. On the other side of the path are Douglas firs, natives of western America, introduced to Britain in 1827. The Woodland Trust have felled much of the conifer plantation to allow natural regeneration. Foxglove leaves are springing up everywhere and there will be a wonderful display of purple foxglove spikes next June.

On the bare banks by the path, our hunters discovered lots of brown, cup fungi; Laura and Robert's book – *Collins' Gem Guide to Fungi* – called them pigs' ears. What an amazing realm is the world of fungi, with ears, clubs, deceivers and tongues – something to excite us all.

DECEMBER

December 22nd 1997

Mary said, "Have you seen my babies?" The first lambs had been born and Mary had moved them, with their mothers, into the field next to our garden. A cold time they had of it, for on Tuesday afternoon it began to snow.

That night we went to Dartington, for a natural history quiz evening. We drove through flurries of snow. By the time we returned – past ten o'clock – the wind had strengthened and the flakes were coming down in earnest, swivelling through the headlight beams of the car in swirling patterns, driven by the wild, easterly wind. Along Slapton Line, shingle and seaweed had been thrown across the road. Near Torcross we stopped and watched the boiling rolls of surf roaring in from the sea and exploding upwards, like volcanic eruptions in the darkness.

The next morning, the fields were a white chequerboard; drifts of snow were piled against the hedge banks. Over the hedge I saw eleven ewes and seventeen, wriggly-tailed lambs – Mary's babies, safe and sound.

The excitement of the snow made it impossible to stay indoors. I walked down the road to the Avon Valley. Across the snow-covered marsh, the ditches showed up black, fringed green with fools' watercress. From the side of a ditch, a small, black bird, with white belly and white rump, flew up, giving a brief piccolo-trill call – a green sandpiper. Rod Bone sees them every winter, down this valley.

The river was rushing, brown and streaked, under the two arches of Hatch Bridge. Near the river bank a dipper was walking in and out of the river. It winked at me, as the white membrane flicked across its eye. By flexing its knees, it curtsied, its white breast turned towards me. After some more walking under water, searching for caddis and stonefly larvae on the river-bed, the dipper flew off upstream, under the bridge.

Walking back up the lane, towards Churchstow, the hedges looked beautiful; the trunks and branches of the trees had white edges and the network of hedgerow twigs had trapped the snow in intricate, cauliflower masses. In one of John Marks' farm gateways, the snow had melted and a flock of birds had gathered to feed. There were sparrows, chaffinches, yellowhammers all jostling for grain and weed seeds from the muddy ground.

After the thaw, I went to Andrew's Wood, to repair the catches on some of the nest boxes. Where we had cleared out last year's birds nests, mice and shrews had taken up residence. From its nest of leaves and shredded grass, a pigmy shrew pushed out his long, velvety nose, sniffed the air and emerged, inquisitively. His coat was dark grey velvet and he was so small. Woodmice were in several of the other boxes. They were much bigger, with big, round eyes. Two poked out their heads and then burrowed back down into their nests. Another took one look at me and leapt, like a kangaroo, out of the box and down onto the woodland floor. I hope he returned when the intruder had gone.

December 21st 1998

'And a song thrush in an oak tree!' It was while walking back home from Kingsbridge that I heard the thrush, in the unofficial nature reserve by Cookworthy Road. This area, with bramble thicket and sapling trees, between the road and the stream that flows from under Plymouth Road, is often full of wildlife. On the other side of the stream, the long strips of garden, belonging to the houses in Fore Street, run down to its edge. Mature trees have grown up and it was from the very top of one of these trees that the song thrush was singing.

On the 1841 map of Kingsbridge the garden plot was owned by 'Mrs Dorville', George Montagu's mistress Eliza Dorville. I hope the area remains wild and rich in wildlife. A pair of goldcrests were fluttering through the bramble clumps, where a yellow-browed warbler had wintered a few years ago.

It was Peter Cummings who started me singing Christmas songs. We covered the west side of the estuary together, for the monthly estuary count. After we had spotted and counted a group of cirl buntings sat in a hedgerow, he added, in a fine tenor voice, "And a partridge in a pear tree." The tune stuck there in my head and wouldn't go away.

The Kingsbridge Estuary in winter.

We could not complete all twelve days of Christmas and many of our counts would have added an unacceptable number of verses; whoever has heard of 'Fifty-four Brent geese gobbling *Zostera* grass'? But we did have 'Twelve cormorants spreading their wings,' perched on the Saltstone.

Walking up Blanksmill Creek, we saw a flock of wigeon, a hundred or more in a curve of the channel, amongst them some pintail were scattered. The drakes were patterned in shades of grey, with elegant, white necks, chocolate brown heads and long, black needle tails. We counted them: 'Nine pintails posing!'

It had been above Lincombe that we had seen the cirl buntings that started it all. The sun was shining on the cirl buntings, showing up the subtle sage-greens, browns and buffs of their plumage. On the males the black markings through the eye and under the chin were clear. And they were 'Eight cirl buntings sun-bathing.'

Number seven were the most attractive of the presents we found for our true-loves. They were dancing and running through the shallow water of Blanksmill Creek, near the lime kiln: 'Seven little egrets tripping lightly.' Where the tide washed over the seaweeds, Peter picked out, through his telescope, 'Six dabchicks diving' and, out on the mud, were the remains of the Collapit family of swans, 'Five swans a-sitting.' The four were 'Greenshank scything,' slashing at the water with their up-turned bills. The three were 'Yellowhammers shining in the sun,' – bright yellow like tropical birds. It was 'Two great crested grebes sailing,' grey-white and stately, swimming past the Saltstone. And finally, a streak of blue over the mud at Collapit – 'And a kingfisher speeding like an arrow.'

December 17th 2002

One of our blue tits is almost black and looks as if it has been checking the chimneys, to warn Father Christmas which are the sootiest. This blue tit is melanistic, meaning it was born with too much black pigment; albinos suffer from a lack of pigment. It is strange that it appeared just before last Christmas and only now has it reappeared. I'll be seeing Santa's reindeer next!

Martin Ranwell joined me on our estuary count and Oliver Smith came to help. Where the stream comes out at the top of Kingsbridge Quay, a little group of ducks and gulls were gathered. The mallards were dabbling their bills to sieve out food from the rushing water. The black-headed gulls were dibbing their red beaks into the mud to pick up morsels from the surface. An egret waded through the water, snatching at fish or opossum shrimps with his slender, black bill. Walking along the mud, by the water's edge, was a redshank, with its orange legs almost hidden by splashes of mud. It was probing its beak into the mud to pull out rag-worms. Over in Tacket Wood creek were several more redshanks walking over the mud and a paler version, nearly as white as a gull, wading through the water like an egret; this was a greenshank.

I never saw the kingfisher. Oliver saw it, shooting low over the water, and Martin spotted it just before it disappeared up towards the Ropewalk Centre.

At the slipway on Embankment Road, we walked down onto the foreshore and round to New Bridge at Bowcombe. Shelduck were spread out over the mud and one pair were very close to us, pushing their beaks through the mud to collect the tiny *Hydrobia* shells, their favourite diet. A curlew, with his down-curved bill, posed for us by the main channel. Shortly afterwards we found a pair of bar-tailed godwits, which have slightly up-tilted bills, walking by the water and pushing their beaks up and down into the mud like a sewing machine needle.

In the channel, two red-breasted mergansers were diving, close enough for us to see the drake's shaggy-crested black head and white neck-ring. Further down the channel a party of about a dozen were fishing together, diving in unison and coming back to the surface in ones and twos.

Far out, at the edge of the mud-flats, about seventy wigeon were drifting in on the rising tide. Then, no more than twenty yards away, a bulky, dark bird with a white throat and breast, surfaced. For a second I caught it in the binoculars, before it submerged with barely a ripple; long enough to see the huge dagger bill and steeply sloping forehead of a great northern diver. For about half an hour we watched it, having some wonderful views.

When we met some of the other counters we found that Michael Brooking, Jim Bennett and Tony Tabb had been watching a great northern diver in Frogmore Creek and Ian Nicholas and Bruce Hall another, near Gerston Point, all at the same time. So we have at least three great northern divers on the estuary.

December 19th 2006

Barbara doesn't know yet. She will say, "I told you so!" and smile. We had argued over a queen wasp, which had fallen out of the sitting room curtains, as we closed them against the dimpsey dark. Barbara had said, "Tread on it." When I protested, she reminded me of the saying of an old friend's grandmother. This Victorian lady had declared herself a Buddhist but insisted that "Wasps and mosquitoes don't count!" But instead of treading on the creature, I had gathered it into my handkerchief and thrown it out of the bathroom window.

The next day I was washing the car before driving to Goveton to help Peter Edwards and Barbara cut down the Christmas tree for Buckland Tout Saints church. We have an outside tap, below the bathroom window and I was fitting a hose to it, to give the car a final rinse. I felt a sudden, piercing pain in my little finger. I had disturbed my queen wasp from her new hiding place behind the tap and she had reacted in the only way she knew.

71

I couldn't admit to Barbara what had happened, so all afternoon, while cutting down and setting up the beautiful Norway spruce in church, I suffered in silence.

Our day in Andrew's Wood was spent clearing some birch, bramble and sallow scrub from the Two Andrews' Clearing. For over thirty years we have been cutting back scrub as it invades the clearings, to keep the variety of habitats and the variety of wildlife. This is a special place that I love. Everything is of value; has a role to play. The grass shelters the insects and the spiders, birch trees, as they begin to rot, provide nest sites for woodpeckers, dormice eat the honeysuckle berries and strip its bark to weave into their nests. Jackie Gage, Devon Wildlife Trust's reserves officer, provided us with a Christmas time treat; not only mince pies but potatoes wrapped in tin foil and roasted on our fire – black but delicious.

Bonfire in Andrew's Wood.

It all reminds me of George Montagu's words, written two hundred years ago but with a message that is so relevant for today: 'Every link in the great chain of nature is important.' Wasps, spiders, toads and even hunter-gatherer humans have their important place.

In so many ways Montagu was a man ahead of his time. I thought 'Xmas' was a modern corruption of the word Christmas but, in a letter he wrote to his friend Robert Anstice in December 1813, George Montagu signed off with, 'Wishing you a merry Xmas and a happy New Year.'" And the same from me to you!